James Withey is the author of the bestselling books *How to Tell Depression to Piss Off: 40 Ways to Get Your Life Back, How to Tell Anxiety to Sod Off: 40 Ways to Get Your Life Back* and *How to Get to Grips with Grief: 40 Ways to Manage the Unmanageable,* and is the co-editor of *The Recovery Letters: Addressed to People Experiencing Depression* and *What I Do to Get Through: How to Run, Swim, Cycle, Sew, or Sing Your Way Through Depression.*

He is the founder of The Recovery Letters project which publishes online letters from people recovering from depression. James trained as a person-centred counsellor and worked in addiction, homelessness and mental health services. He lives with depression and anxiety and writes and speaks about mental health. He lives in Hove in the UK with his husband and emotionally damaged cat. You can find him at www.jameswithey.com.

Also by James Withey

How to Tell Depression to Piss Off
How to Tell Anxiety to Sod Off
How to Get to Grips with Grief

How to Smash Stress

40 Ways to Get Your Life Back

James Withey

ROBINSON

ROBINSON

First published in Great Britain in 2023 by Robinson

1 3 5 7 9 10 8 6 4 2

Important Note
This book is not intended as a substitute for medical advice or treatment.
Any person with a condition requiring medical attention should consult a
qualified medical practitioner or suitable therapist.

A CIP catalogue record for this book is available from the British Library.

ISBN: 978-1-47214-776-9

Typeset in Sentinel by Initial Typesetting Services, Edinburgh
Printed and bound in Great Britain by Clays Ltd, Elcograf S.p.A

Papers used by Robinson are from well-managed forests and other responsible sources.

Robinson
An imprint of
Little, Brown Book Group
Carmelite House
50 Victoria Embankment
London EC4Y 0DZ

An Hachette UK Company
www.hachette.co.uk

www.littlebrown.co.uk

How To Books are published by Robinson, an imprint of
Little, Brown Book Group. We welcome proposals from
authors who have first-hand experience of their subjects.
Please set out the aims of your book, its target market
and its suggested contents in an email to
howto@littlebrown.co.uk

For Fiona B

'It won't be awful for always.'

Contents

Introduction

Stress is a hideous, infectious, spreading rash.

Living with it is all-consuming. It seeps into every part of your life until it's all you can think about. It impacts every sinew of your mind and body. It will take you down unless you apply some high-strength cream pretty quickly.

It's hard to find your way out of stress. You can't see how it will get easier or when it will get easier or what you need to do to make it easier. You just want it to go so you can breathe again, have some room in your head again. Start living again.

I know this rash. I know how utterly debilitating it is. I have been so stressed I became convinced it would never end, that it was all my fault, that it was just me being unable to manage life.

I would desperately hope that somehow, I would have the fortune to turn into the Dalai Lama, or maybe Buddha, or one of those people on Instagram who drink a bottle of kiwi and alfalfa juice and seem to float through life like a cloud, turning each and every stressor into a way of becoming more at one with the earth.

The things is, there are three pillars in our lives that help keep us stable. Home, work and relationships. If one of the pillars becomes shaky, has a chip in it or starts to crack, then we experience stress.

When one of my pillars (or sometimes two or all three) started to wobble I would wake in the middle of the night, unable to sleep, ruminating about each and every problem in my life, trying to think about how I could get it under control.

If only I could get myself together, I would say to myself. Man up. Be more stoic and resilient, then it would be okay. Spoiler: it didn't work. I've learned the hard way that what you *think* might be the right thing to do often isn't.

When you try and manage your stress and it doesn't work, the rash comes back even stronger because you still feel stressed, but on top of that you feel even more stressed because your stress management techniques didn't work. And you have to be very careful because stress can exacerbate pre-existing conditions like depression, anxiety and panic attacks.

You can't function with a debilitating rash all over you, so we have to find ways to get it under control.

After reading this book you'll have tools to keep it at

bay. And fear not, I'm not going to suggest you just do some deep breathing and imagine you're a tranquilised squirrel.

You have to apply these tools regularly to keep that rash under control because unlike the people who drink kiwi and alfalfa juice, life events and stress never go away, what changes is our ability to manage them.

Also, managing stress is a doing thing, rather than a sit back on a deckchair and eat a strawberry ice-cream thing, which is a bugger, but it's best that we're aware of that before we begin. We can't just wish stress away, and often it won't go away by itself; we have to *do* things.

However, I give you express permission to eat an ice-cream of your choice whilst tackling your stress. I'll have rum and raisin (which is the best ice-cream flavour in the world, and no, I won't be entertaining any other views on this). Also, thank you very much for paying; very kind of you.

The good news is there are forty different ways to try to reduce your stress levels in this book. You can try one at a time or try a few together. If one doesn't work, don't worry, just try another, and you can always go back and try the first one at another time.

Oh, and I haven't just made these ways up off the top of my head. I didn't think, 'Hmm . . . I don't know, maybe eating quiche? Yes, eating quiche might be good for stress, I'll make that a chapter.'

These are tried and tested ways. I've tried them and used them, and I've worked with others who've tried and use them too. They've been double-checked, actually triple-checked because I asked my cat too, but he suggested I give him huge quantities of tuna, so he can't be wholly relied upon.

They work for me, they work for others and they'll work for you too. If they don't, I'll buy you a pet pygmy goat called Belinda.*

The chapters are short so you can start putting the ways in place really quickly and the book isn't too long, so you won't feel even more stressed about having to finish a six-hundred-page book on top of everything else.

Also, you don't need to start at the beginning like a traditional book. Start in the middle; start at the end and work backwards; flick through the book and just choose a chapter at a time – whatever works for you.

I'm going to use some humour in this book to lighten things up a bit and make the book easier to read. The last thing you need at the moment is an overly serious book that will bring your mood down further.

We're going to get through this.

Let's smash stress, together.

James

*I may not actually buy you a pet pygmy goat called Belinda, sorry.

1. You're not actually a superhero

In case you didn't realise it, you're not a superhero.

Admittedly, you do look *superb* wearing underpants over a pair of bright red tights, but that's as far as it goes, I'm afraid.

You can't shoot spider webs from the palm of your hand. That purple cloak you inherited from Great Uncle Arthur won't let you levitate to forty thousand feet and fly between New York City skyscrapers. You can't lift up three double decker buses with one finger, and those cheap sunglasses from the supermarket you brought a few years ago won't make you invisible.

(Call me if you want any further self-esteem and confidence boosters, I'm always here for you.)

A few years ago, I was walking down the street, because I didn't know what else to do. My job had become so overwhelming it was all I could think about. However much work I did each day, I seemed to get nothing done.

More work seemed to create more work. I'd snap at the staff, snap at my boss, snap at my husband and snap at my friends. I was basically a crocodile at this point.

I started to regret taking the promotion which gave me about another twenty pence a month after tax and what I got in return was a whole heap of stress. What was I thinking? Why didn't I stay in my old job? I would have been twenty pence poorer but happier and not having nightmares about unsent emails and missed deadlines.

Most days after work I would come home, smoke cigarettes and drink too much wine. I couldn't eat, I couldn't sleep, I couldn't watch television. My life was my stress; stress was my life.

As I passed other people on the street, I looked at them and thought, 'I wish I was them. They look carefree, they don't look so stressed that they're thinking about running away to Antarctica and living with the penguins. They seem to be managing their stress, not imagining how to disguise themselves as a flightless aquatic bird.'

I sat down on a wall outside a betting shop. I should be more stoic, I thought, I should be more resilient, like a superhero. I should be able to handle this.

Instead of turning into Spider-Man (or a penguin), I'd turned into Stephen the 'Should Monster'. His superpower is to make you feel crap about how you're managing your stress. I don't think Marvel comics are going to be chasing me for copyright any time soon, because all he does is scream at you, 'You should be stronger,' which offers limited storyline options.

What I didn't realise then, which I realise now, is that it wasn't a case of needing to be more stoic, or resilient or stronger. It was a case of accepting that I was massively struggling, and not trying to tell myself to 'buck up' like a Victorian father to his son whose just lost his leg in a tram accident.

7

'Buck up' gets you nowhere. It just makes you feel worse about yourself, worse that you can't manage your stress, and then worse again because it doesn't improve the stress you're experiencing.

In the end I limped along in the job for too long. I got even more stressed, I kept drinking too much, smoking too much, harming my relationships and eventually got another job; but not before it had taken a huge toll on my physical and mental health.

So let's be clear. **You're not a flipping superhero**. That's in bold which means it's important.

You're human. All humans experience stress. You struggle but struggling does NOT mean that you're any less worthy as a person or a penguin.

Boring and tedious as being a human can be sometimes, it's what we are, and we're not made to be in a state of high alert and terror all the time. It damages us, like, really, really, badly.

It's better that we accept our limitations and realise we're not made to be a superhero. You have to learn to manage your own expectations of yourself. Don't try to be perfect with ideals that you can never live up to.

Okay, so you didn't get that promotion; someone else did. Maybe your relationship failed, or you've fallen out with a long-term friend, but none of these things mean you're a failure as a person. Let's just read that again together – that doesn't mean you're a failure as a person. You have to practise telling yourself this, because stress will tell you the opposite.

When we let go of trying to be perfect and just try to be good enough, a lot of our stress recedes. Trying to be stoic is the worst thing you can do to manage your stress.

If you rile against your stress and spend your whole time ruminating and thinking you should be 'stronger', then you'll fixate on that and won't prioritise tackling what's causing the actual stress.

I know this because I can ruminate for the nation. My mind will go, 'I should be able to manage this', 'Why aren't I managing this better?' and 'It's not that big a deal really, is it?'

All of this wastes time and gets us nowhere.

Ultimately, what I'm saying here is stop giving yourself

a bloody, frigging hard time about experiencing stress. That's an order.

I'm being all bossy and everything because it's important. I'm also giving you a hard stare, and this particular hard stare even beat Paddington Bear in the 'International Hard Stare' competition in Peru.

Accepting that you're stressed and naming what you're experiencing as stress is also vital to tackling it. Therefore, try and say to yourself, 'I'm experiencing a lot of stress,' rather than 'I'm stressed,' as the latter places emphasis on personal failure. You haven't failed as a person; you're just being human.

Now, I'll let you try on the tights and underpants combination one more time, and then no more superhero fantasies, okay?

9

2. Don't make sudden decisions and don't buy purple flippers

I'm not a psychiatrist, psychologist, neurologist, or any other profession ending with 'ist'. But I do know stress. Maybe that makes me a stress-ist? Ooh, I may have just made up a new profession.

When we're stressed, we want the stress to go away. We want quick solutions; we frantically look for ways to solve the problem and that can cause us to make decisions that are often bad for us in the long run.

Decisions become especially bad at four o'clock in the morning when we think the solution is to resign from a job, put the house up for sale, end the relationship or, in my case, buy purple diving flippers on eBay.

It's all part of our inbuilt fight or flight instincts leftover from the days when we had to flee from hordes of marauding thugs from the next village, coming to attack us with oversized clubs and making threatening 'ugghhh' sounds. We feel that we have to do something and do it quickly.

But to deal with stress we have to have a clear head, and my purple flippers are a permanent reminder of the perils of making hasty decisions when I'm stressed.

I bought them because I thought they would allow the staff I managed to see my light-hearted side. To be fair, it was a fancy dress do for charity, but I was so stressed that I hadn't prepared a costume and so obviously showing up in my suit and purple flippers would be just the ticket. Utter hilarity would ensue, and they would all love me. Needless to say, this didn't happen. There was just lots of 'Oh gosh, so . . . what – I mean, yes . . . so, what have you actually come as James?'

11

After about eight o'clock in the evening our brains start to slow down and think about sleep. So, don't even consider making any decisions between then and eight o'clock in the morning, okay? That's why the old saying of 'sleep on it first' holds so much truth.

Those who originated that saying (whoever they were) knew a thing or two and it pays to listen to them. You don't want to be landed with unwanted aquatic purple footwear.

Nor do you want to make a decision that you're going to regret. You want to make informed decisions when your brain is in a calmer, clearer state.

When it gets to eight o'clock I turn my computer off. I don't decide to fly to Ulan Bator to visit the Gandantegchinlen Monastery, however much I want to. I don't text a friend who I've fallen out with. I don't put the flat up for sale. I don't buy a holiday home on the Albanian Riveria.

When I was a teenager, I worked as a waiter in a restaurant at a caravan park before going to university. I was on shift every Saturday and Sunday lunchtime directing the caravaners to the carvery – and that was it. That was my job. I cleared a few plates, smiled at people, but essentially, I was a glorified theatre usher, but with more roast potatoes involved. It was a cushy and surprisingly well-paid job, and I got to eat a ridiculous number of leftover desserts.

Then the manager asked if I'd like to work during the week as well as the weekend lunchtimes. Despite having no real waiting experience, and no ability to do mental arithmetic – this was *way* before tills that worked out the bill for you and you could pay via card or phone, you understand. The 1800s were a tough period for us mathematically challenged folk – I thought, 'That sounds like a great idea. More cash, more free dessert.'

The kitchen was home to one of those stereotypical really angry chefs who would scream at me for getting the orders wrong as my handwriting was also terrible. Glenda the manager thought she was running afternoon tea at the Ritz, rather than a café in a converted stable in a rundown caravan park, in a remote part of Dorset.

After a few weeks I'd had enough. The stress was too much. I phoned the manager of the Ritz (aka Glenda the Merciless) and handed my notice in. Did I want to keep my weekend job and not do the weekdays, she asked? 'No,' I replied. 'Absolutely not. I don't want to work with any of you ever, ever again, ever, EVER.' I had a penchant for the dramatic when I was seventeen. Did I want to think about it and get back to her in a few days, she asked. 'Definitely not. I have had enough. I am worth more than this. Okay, so I get all the orders wrong, I need to have a calculator in my back pocket and the chef can't tell if I've written down tomato toastie or strawberry pavlova, but still the answer is no, always will be no. NO, NO, NO.'

Needless to say, I regretted my decision. Not least because of the free desserts but also the lack of essential beer money when I went to university – or, if my mum is reading this, the lack of money for fruit, vegetables, textbooks and clean socks.

We have to be careful because stress pushes us into making bad decisions.

Sometimes we have to let things develop a bit. Waiting it out doesn't always feel like a tactic to manage stress but it's effective because it allows time for things to change and for your brain to clear so you can make better choices.

If in doubt, talk to someone who knows you well, who sees the situation objectively and who is also not stressed – otherwise there will be two of you making bad decisions. Look at different options together, make a list if you want so you can clearly see the options available to you.

3. Dude, what's within your control?

A conversation with my friend Jess over coffee and bagels in a local café.

ME: I'm so stressed, I can't cope with this life stuff. Why do we have to become adults? Why can't I just stay in my childhood bedroom with my posters and books and someone – maybe you – can just come round with food and cocktails and stuff.

JESS: Because you're thirty-eight and need to grow up.

ME: Don't be horrible and nasty you big ploppy poo face.

JESS: I think you're proving my point.

ME: It's all getting on top of me. I'm a lost ship on a stormy sea destined to wash up on the rocks and be torn apart.

JESS: It's great you're not being too dramatic about things.

ME: I have to pack up the house, we can't find

anywhere to live, the bank is on top of me about that loan, the car failed its MOT and I'm waiting on the test results from the hospital.

JESS: Anything else?

ME: They didn't put enough marmite on this bagel.

JESS: That's an entirely good thing because marmite is an abomination.

ME: You heretic! I hate you.

JESS: Listen, just stop for a second. Dude, tell me what's within your control?

ME: What do you mean, 'What's within your control'? And did you just call me dude?

JESS: Dude, if you finish that bagel with the revolting black devil spread on it, dude, I'll explain, dude.

ME: Fine, but for the love of God, stop calling me dude. [*I finish the bagel*]

JESS: Right, I want you to tell me all the things in your life that you DO have control over.

ME: Okay, I don't see why this is useful, but I guess I can control my spending? Is that what you mean?

JESS: Great, anything else?

ME: Umm . . . I can try and control my hatred of you for not liking marmite.

JESS: Either do this properly or I'm going to throw my cappuccino in your face.

ME: Fine. Fine. So, I guess I can control my actions in relation to other things. I can say no to things. I can control where I go. I can make choices about what I eat. I can choose what to wear, when to go to bed.

JESS: Great, take a breath and reflect on all those things for a second. [A *few seconds pass*] How do you feel now?

ME: I don't want to say.

JESS: [*Sighing*] I suspect you're feeling slightly freer because you realise that you're not a lost ship in a stormy sea; you have stress but you also have choices. Remembering the things you can control at the moment will allow you to make better decisions about your stress and not feel so trapped.

ME: Yeah, I suppose. You're still wrong about marmite though.

So, this is what I do when I'm feeling stressed. I count all the things I *do* have control over to make me realise I'm not just a ship being bounced around in the sea.

Stress is often about all the things we don't have control over, so, as Jess says, by concentrating on all the things we *do* have control over it makes managing the stressors easier.

You have to balance things up to be able to see more clearly what you need to do, otherwise you feel like that ship on the sea with no control at all – which just isn't true.

4. Slowwwww everything dowwwnnnn

Please do me a favour and slow the hell down.

Slow your thoughts down, slow your actions down, slow your movements down, slow your conversations down, make some sloe gin and find a slow worm. The last two are optional.

When I'm stressed everything speeds up, I even wee really fast. Maybe that was too much information?

It's partly because at times my stress is caused by having so much to do and I flitter around like a white-throated swift on cheap cocaine. Partly it's because I think if I keep moving, the reality of how difficult things are won't catch up with me.

A few years ago, my relationship had split up. I was dumped by someone I thought I would spend the rest of my life with, but it turned out he was just an asshole – so often the case, isn't it? At the time it felt like the worst thing to happen. I was also struggling to pay my rent, working two incredibly low paid jobs (hating them both) and my cat had just died.

Each day I would oversleep because I was so tired, then make a dash for the shower, run for the train – miss the train, get the next train, speed around at work making coffee for ungrateful people, cry in the staff room at lunch-time manically texting my ex telling him it was all my fault, and would he have me back? Then, dash to the train to go to my evening job – miss the train, get the next train, scurry around serving food to ungrateful people, cry in the staff room about my cat, head home (high on caffeine and adrenalin) and repeat it all the next day.

I had to slow down. Not least because my blood was 94 per cent Guatemalan Maragogype Elephant Coffee.

I suspect that, at the moment, you're either feeling like there aren't enough hours in the day or that all the hours that you do have are consumed with worry. Am I right? If I am, buy me a decaf coffee, which is all I can drink these days.

When we slow everything down it allows room for stress to be seen more clearly and tackled more effectively.

You can't manage stress whilst simultaneously doing the weekly food shop, dog-sitting next door's spaniel, sending work emails on your phone, fending off text messages from your children asking for triple chocolate and caramel mousse for pudding, and trying to get the app for

19

your bank to open on your phone after being locked out for the fifteenth time because you forgot that your password was the name of next door's spaniel.

Whilst we keep running and chasing our tails, stress will increase and the amount of time to manage it will decrease and things will get worse.

You have to slow down.

It will seem counter-intuitive initially, but trust me on this one, it will help. When we move slower, think slower, take time to act rather than react, stress improves.

You know when you're in a busy station running for your train, and everyone is in the way so you start running faster because you think it will get you to the train quicker, but what actually happens is that by charging ahead you bump into people, you lose your way, you can't keep track of the platform change, you shout, 'Get out of my way you sodding, sodding imbeciles,' and then get arrested for public disturbance. No? Well, you get my point. The faster you move the less you achieve, and it's the same with stress. In order to manage it effectively you have to be more considered, plan your route more carefully and not be a hot-headed liability.

5. Escape! Escape!

Once when I was so stressed, I ran away from home.

It wasn't the most mature thing I've ever done but it was the most understandable, because when we're stressed, we want to escape.

Somehow, I felt that if I kept running, I would eventually leave my stress behind. I wasn't actually running you understand, as I would've only got to the end of the road and then passed out due to lack of oxygen. Instead, I got on a train and headed out of town.

I needed to flee, escape, go west, leave behind all the crap and start again. I would build a wooden house in the forest, find some squirrels to be my friends, grow vegetables, eat berries from the hedgerow and never have to speak to or interact with another human being again. It would be great. Without people or things I wouldn't have any stress so everything would be sorted. No relationships. No work worries. No grief.

The flaw in my plan was that I can't hit a nail straight

into a wall, let alone build a house. Squirrels have never been particularly friendly towards me (some have been downright hostile). When I tried to grow tomatoes, the slugs ate them overnight. I also can't identify a poison berry from a blackberry, and I quite like people, well, some of them. I like you, for instance.

The train went to London where there's some sort of law against building wooden houses in Hyde Park, so I had an ice-cream and came home. Even if I had found somewhere to build a wooden house I would have worried about leaks in the roof, the carrots being eaten by rabbits and the antagonistic characteristics of squirrels.

It's fine to feel that we want to escape but, and I'm going to be a bit strict about this, don't do it. You can tell me to 'piss off', it's fine, I can take it. Just let me explain.

As much as we want to run away when we're stressed, our worries are devilishly pernicious, and they follow us. They stick to us like paparazzi following an A-list celebrity sex scandal.

Escaping isn't just physical. We want to create escape in our minds as well.

When I got my first job as a manager, in a homelessness service, I was incredibly stressed. I couldn't stay on top of the work. I constantly worried about the staff and the people we were supporting. The only thing that seemed to help was a bottle of red wine when I got home. Well, it helped in the sense that for a few hours I no longer cared about my stress and was more interested in texting all my friends telling them how much I loved them.

It didn't solve my work stress at all because I would wake up hungover, and all the problems hadn't miraculously disappeared because I bought a nice bottle of Châteauneuf-du-Pape.

It could be alcohol, but it could be other drugs. Shopping or over-exercising or gambling or binge eating or anything else that could potentially cause you harm physically, psychologically or financially.

23

Now, don't get me wrong, sometimes a gin and tonic or a bottle of cold Slovenian lager (try them, they're great) totally hits the spot. The problem comes when you start relying on these things to manage your stress.

The bugger of it all is that you can never truly escape your stress; you have to head into it. Escaping equals delaying and the stress won't go anywhere just because you keep relying on those Balkan yeast-fermented beverages.

The trick is to recognise *when* you're trying to escape, be it on a train or in your mind, put the brakes on and try a different strategy.

6. Get a stress buddy

I have an imaginary friend called Beth.

I realise that imaginary friends are mostly confined to six-year-old children, but Beth is my buddy and very useful she is too.

She's calm, practical, has oodles of common sense, she's objective and compassionate. When I'm really stressed, I think, what would Beth say and then have an imaginary conversation with her.

She has effortlessly cool style – wears classic vintage clothes that if anyone else wore them they'd look like children's dressing-up clothes. She has these glasses which she picked up in a Parisian flea market that make her look urbane and sophisticated. She owns a contemporary art gallery but also won a Nobel prize for physics a few years ago.

Here is a conversation between Beth and me. She's wearing her cool glasses, I'm wearing glasses too, but they're not quite as cool.

ME: I can't cope with everything; Alex is really unwell and I don't know what to do. I have so many emails my inbox has stopped counting them and just says 'way too many'. I have to go to a wedding at the other end of the country with people I hate and . . . oh, oh no, for the love of God, no, NO, please no, no, NOOOOOO . . . Not now, why *now* of all times?

BETH: What's happened?

ME: Sweet mercy upon my tortured soul, forsooth I may have sinned but surely my worth is greater than my transgressions?

BETH: James, you've started to speak in Old English again, just tell me what's happened?

ME: The cat's been a little bit sick on the carpet.

BETH: So your arm hasn't fallen off then?

ME: No.

BETH: Go and clean it up and then come back.

ME: Right, I'm back. Sorry.

BETH: That's okay. Now, I think it's best if we tackle one thing at a time. Is that okay?

ME: Yes, Beth.

BETH: Right, so this wedding. Do you really need to go?

ME: I do really but I don't want to.

BETH: Do you hate everyone who's going?

ME: Mostly. Well, not everyone.

BETH: Right, then may I suggest that you spend time with the people you don't despise and realise that going to a wedding is for the couple not you. They want you there otherwise they wouldn't have invited you, and a few hours' possible discomfort is nothing to make them happy on the most important day of their life.

ME: Yeah, okay, fair enough.

BETH: Next your emails. So, you need a strict prioritisation system, delete all the nonsense you're getting in, unsubscribe from those mailing lists for 'instant grey hair rejuvenation' and that arts cinema you went to in Moldova. Then develop a flag order for what needs to be done daily, weekly or monthly and stick to it.

ME: But that will take a lot of work.

BETH: Yes, but you're not getting any work done so you need to spend some time getting things organised so that you *can* get some work done.

ME: Fine, fine.

BETH: Next, Alex. You don't have the power to magically heal people from their illnesses. I think you should know that by now. You have to support him through his illness, offer to go to the hospital with him, send videos of ducks on slides, make bad jokes and listen when he needs to be heard. You need to be there for him, not think you can try and cure him.

ME: I guess. It's just that it's so unfair and—

BETH: Life is. It's unfair for everyone, we all suffer, it sucks and the sooner you get your head around that the more you can see the immense joy in life too.

ME: Mistress, I must thank thee for thy cunning and expedience.

BETH: Just stop. Please.

Beth is the logical part of my brain that I find hard to access when in the middle of the whirlwind that is stress.

Somehow imagining conversations with her allows me to see what I should do, to calm myself down and move forward. It's a bit weird but it totally works, and because it's helpful and it doesn't harm anyone, I keep doing it (and weirdness is great in my book).

You don't have to call your stress buddy Beth, but they need to have a name that you don't associate with anyone. It's good to have a strong sounding, no-nonsense name, so Finn Flimsy Featherlight may not cut it.

And yes, it might feel a bit odd initially to be creating a stress buddy and having imaginary conversations with them but just try it – what have you got to lose apart from some stress?

Beth always encourages me to make to-do lists and create plans to tackle my problems. She is the practical, sensible part of me that I can't always access when I'm stressed. And she rocks.

7. That's AWESOME!

Where were we? Oh, yes, mountains. Okay, we weren't talking about mountains, but we're going to. And lakes and seas and hills and fields and valleys and stuff.

We have to find ways to shrink stress because otherwise it will loom over you, grow bigger and bigger, until it's all you are – which is probably how you're feeling at the moment.

You know those vacuum-packed meals you get where all the air is taken out? Well, that's what we're going to do with stress, shrink wrap it. We do that by getting awe into our lives.

When we experience big awe-inspiring things, stress gets smaller by comparison. I want you to see and experience things that make you go, 'Bleedin' hell, that's FRIGGING AWESOME.' That's the plan.

I'm not a great mountain climber in all honesty, if there were escalators to the top of them (and why aren't there?), then I would happily be on them, rather than walking up. But the views I love. The views and grandeur are everything to me.

I once went on holiday in Norway when I was incredibly stressed. There were problems with my friends and family and tension everywhere – people not talking to one another, fights, arguments and general crapness all around. I had no idea what to do or how to make things better.

I was in two minds about going away with so much stress. How would I be able to relax? Would I just be thinking about all the stress and not be able to enjoy myself? But my husband persuaded me to go and on the first morning we ended up at the top of a mountain, via a handy funicular (God bless the Norwegians).

A few feet away from the exit we came to the edge of the mountain and suddenly an enormous vista of fjords, mountains, forests, valleys and sea opened up. It took my breath away. The sheer scale of the countryside, the expanse of green, the delicious intersecting patchwork of water and trees. It was incredible. We both stood with our mouths open and suddenly all the pettiness of bickering and gossiping started to shrink. What did that matter when there was all this? It was all so small in comparison. So insignificant.

We walked down the mountain (via a handy path, we didn't abseil obviously) and were still gobsmacked; the intensity of my stress shrank even further. It all became so much less important. I almost skipped down the path to the bottom. I didn't, of course, because this would have been the perfect moment for the universe to have taught me a lesson and tripped me up, but there was a lightness to my mind and body (and my bank balance too, because the kiosk on top of the mountain charged twelve pounds for a coffee).

It didn't remove the stress – this wasn't a magical mountain after all – but it repositioned it. Beforehand I was sat on the front seat at the cinema, immersed in the action film, consumed by it, surrounded by noise and mayhem, and now I had moved right to the very back; I was still seeing the film but with a different view, more distant, more context – my outlook was so different.

It's all about getting this type of awe into your life when you're stressed. Now, you don't need to head up a Norwegian mountain funicular to do this. Head to a park and look up at an enormous tree. Go to the sea and watch each wave, go to a lake or river and gaze out. Head into a wood and count all the trees. Go to a butterfly farm and see how bizarre and beautiful and wonderful nature is. Something that makes you go 'wow'.

Big nature puts stress into context and suddenly the fact that Brendan from finance has messed up your payslip for the thirteenth time and you have to make an official complaint about him is less important.

Remember it won't remove the causes of your stress, but awe will put the stress into perspective, and you also get to see lovely things so it's a winner all round.

8. Don't feed the stress monster

Stress is a hungry monster.

I realise that sounds like the beginning of a children's picture book, but it's true.

Stress loves being fed with anxiety, worry, rumination and procrastination. It adores eating all the negative stuff you feel with your stress. The more it's fed, the bigger stress gets, so you have to be really careful.

I was about to start a new job and my stress levels were off the chart. I'm not sure which type of chart it was but they were definitely off it. It was a new role I hadn't done before, it was a different commute, new people and a charity I hadn't worked with before.

The months before I started were hideous; worrying about what my boss would think of me and imagining that I would be sacked on the spot for wearing the wrong trousers. I visualised the staff at the end of my first week with pitchforks screaming, 'Get out James! You can't do this job, you moron! Get out now or we'll set the dogs on ya.'

I was convinced I would make so many mistakes the whole organisation would collapse. There would be a public investigation and all the major newspapers would run the headline 'IDIOT JAMES RUINS BELOVED CHARITY', with a picture of me in dark glasses fighting off the paparazzi outside my front door.

I spent hours talking to friends and family about how awful it was going to be, how stressed I was, how it was the wrong decision, how I should never ever, ever be allowed to apply for any other jobs ever, ever again. I listened to music that made me sad, I dwelt on all the mistakes I'd made in my life. I finally decided it was probably best if I moved to the Faroe Islands and became a sheep.

I have a tendency to catastrophise, as no doubt you can see, and it all made my stress so much worse.

You see, I was feeding the stress monster.

I was feeding it so much it got bigger and bigger and bigger, so much so it needed to go and buy new pants it was now so huge. The stress monster wasn't just getting a slice of bread and jam per day, I was giving it a gargantuan banquet fit for an emperor every few hours.

The thing is, your response to stress may make your stress worse.

By the time the first day at the job came around I was a

33

mess of sweat and gibbering incoherence. I hid in the train station toilet for forty-five minutes trying to get a grip. The toll it had taken was huge.

I somehow got through the first day by grinning inanely and instantly forgetting the name and job title of everyone I was introduced to, where my boss's office was, how to switch on my computer and how to get out of the building. The stress had made the first day so much worse than it should have been because I was feeding the monster.

Have a think about a time when the worry about something was worse than the actual thing. When your panic and nerves and dread fed your stress. Perhaps it was going to a party where you only knew the host. Starting a new course, being a best man at a wedding, giving a presentation. How much did the stress you felt beforehand actually help? I'm guessing not much.

Planning helps, preparation helps, practice helps, self-compassion helps, getting support helps. Increasing your stress, raising your anxiety even more, lowering your mood definitely does not.

The thing is, worry doesn't help; taking the right action does. Starve the monster.

9. You can't control other people (as much as you'd like to)

When I'm stressed, I have this wonderful recurring fantasy of buying an island in the Pacific Ocean, surviving on fishfinger sandwiches and passion fruit yoghurt, befriending the local wildlife to keep me company, and living in a lavish manor house by the sea.

Okay, so I may not have thought through all the practical details as all I've ever caught was a crab, when I was eight – I was so scared I dropped it back immediately into the harbour. I mean, they have claws that snap at you in a nasty way – what's that about?

It's a really lovely dream when things are bad and it's so lovely because there aren't any people there. 'Hell is other people' said the famous French philosopher Jean-Paul Sartre, but I also say it (ever so slightly less famous) when I'm stressed.

After a particularly hideous time with friendships in my first year at university, I'd had enough. One person wasn't talking to another, that other person was saying that a third person was saying horrid things to a fourth person, a fifth person was continually ghosting the first person at the student union, and I was having a stress-induced meltdown as only an eighteen-year-old who's just left home can. I could barely follow the plot of an Australian soap opera let alone keep up with the exploits of my friendship group.

In a rash decision (which can only be attributed to far too many pints of lager in the local pub one evening), I decided to try and sort things out, once and for all – I would clear the air and then everything would be fine.

I gathered everyone together in the back room of the local hostelry which I had purloined for the occasion, with the promise of free drinks and crisps to share. I paced around like Poirot ready to unveil the murderer to all the suspects.

'The thing is, we all just have to get along. So, let's just be honest and speak our truths and everything will be sorted,' I said smiling hopefully. 'I truly believe we can get this resolved and move forward into a brighter future.'

'But she kissed Fran when I said I liked them.'

'I did not. I kissed Ryan.'

'You were drunk – that wasn't Ryan, that was Bailey.'

'I knew you liked Bailey. I knew it!'

'You told me you were never going to speak to Bailey again.'

'You complete sodding liar. I never said that.'

'Well, I heard you say that.'

'I heard you too. I also saw you.'

'You didn't see them. I was with you all day and you saw nothing.'

'You always do this.'

'*You* always do this.'

'Right, James, I've had enough of this.'

'Me too. What a ridiculous idea, James.'

'Yeah, James, I'm off as well. Idiot.'

'I'm going too. Honestly, James.'

'See you, James. Thanks for making things worse. Er . . . can I still have my free drink?'

I was left holding my pint, somewhat bewildered, but I'd had my first lesson in not being able to control what other people do or say.

Knowing this helps you manage stress. You only have control of what *you* do, unless you're being controlled by an ancient magic spell, but my hunch is, you're not.

Once you realise and accept that people will say or do what the hell they want, it releases you from the stress of trying to get them to do things differently.

I couldn't make my friends tell the truth, apologise to

each other or start to love each other as fellow earth dwell-
ers – to be honest, it was rather arrogant to think that I
could. Once I relinquished the need to try and control the
situation, and concentrated on what *I* could do, things got
a lot easier and crucially, my stress decreased massively.

It's like trying to get a cat to do an impersonation of
Elvis Presley – it can't be done, and trust me I've spent
many hours trying. He couldn't even master the first verse
of 'Hound Dog' but I'm attributing this to the canine title
and him being a bit scared.

It's like those endless arguments you see on social
media. I no longer engage in them because the likelihood is
that I'm not going to change anyone's mind and the result
will just be me getting more stressed. It puts me back in
control and stops me getting exhausted trying to change
other people all the time.

When you realise you can't control everyone, and concentrate on you – how you respond, what you say, what you
do – it releases a pressure valve. It frees you up and this is
crucial when managing your stress.

10. Smash stuff (and scream)

One afternoon, a few years ago now, my husband found me
smashing cups and plates in the garden.

It's happened to us all right? You walk out of the kitchen
door and find your loved one screaming and destroying
crockery.

HIM: What the flaming hell are you doing?

[*smash*]

ME: I'm cuddling Labrador puppies! What the hell does
it look like I'm doing?

HIM: Why on earth are you smashing things and where
did you get all this stuff?

[*smash*]

ME: Charity shop.

[*smash, smash, smash*]

HIM: Okay, admittedly this is a shocking, terribly
designed 1980s dinner service, but what did it ever do

to you and why are you screaming?

ME: I'm smashing my stress.

HIM: You're doing what, sorry?

ME: I'm stressed.

HIM: I know.

ME: So, I'm smashing it.

HIM: Okay, weird boy. And the screaming?

ME: All part of it.

HIM: Fine, fine. Well, you can explain all this to the police after the neighbours report you.

ME: Smashing, thank you.

HIM: Just don't hit me. Or the cat. And if you hit your-self don't come running to me.

ME: I won't.

HIM: Also, make sure that gravy boat is well and truly broken, it's beyond revolting.

ME: Will do.

[smash]

You don't need to smash a set of neon and puce dishes from the '80s, loads of other things help. Chopping wood, breaking glass, punching a pillow – do it safely, of course, but try it.

Much of our stress is held in our body so when we physically release it, it's a really effective tool to manage what's happening.

You can smash and thump and rip and tear – anything that helps. You could put a picture of your boss's face onto a cushion and throw it across the room. Then throw it across the room again. Then throw it across the room again. Then throw it across the room again. Repeat as necessary.

41

It's okay to feel hate and resentment. If we deny those feelings, it doesn't do good things to us. So, if you feel angry because of your stress, it's got to come out. Sure, there might be some sort of law against actually putting your boss's face onto a cushion and throwing it across the room, but anything that's legal and doesn't harm anyone, go for it. I do.

Also, screaming whilst you smash or thump or pummel something is really, really important to this whole process. It's about physically getting as much stress out as you can.

Swearing is greatly encouraged as well. I mean, really swear, don't hold back at all; you're not a delicate Regency noblewoman who faints when someone says 'stocking', so really let yourself go.

Other additions can be made too. I listen to loud music with earphones on. The kind of music I usually hate when it seeps out of someone's phone on a train journey because of the hideous thumping and shouting, but it works brilliantly for this.

Keep the stress you're experiencing in your mind and then releassseeee.

Get your rage on! It feels really good.

11. Your time starts ... now

I'm in a relationship I hate and I'm really regretting it.

I know it's not right, that we have nothing in common and now he's pressing for us to move in together, relocate to London and eventually get married. It's become smothering and claustrophobic and I don't know what to do.

I've tried to gently tell him that I think we're better off not being together, but this seems to have no impact and he keeps texting me. One day he just shows up at my flat. Without any warning he's just got a plane from London to Glasgow, where I'm living.

I'm giving myself a really hard time. How did I end up in this situation? Have I been misleading or sending mixed messages? I don't want to hurt him but it's all feeling too much.

I love reading and he hates books. I love travelling and he refuses to leave the country. He's obsessed with football, and I've never been able to kick any ball and make it go in the direction I want it to. Most importantly I love

43

yoghurt and he thinks it's the devils breakfast – if the other things weren't the deal breaker, the yoghurt definitely would be.

I'm so stressed I dread every phone call, every text message and now that he's shown up at my flat, I have to put the Timeline Plan in place.

Okay, I know the Timeline Plan isn't a particular sexy title, but I can't think of anything else to call it, apart from TLP, which just sounds a bit like TCP which I had to gargle with as a child when I had a sore throat.

Stress seems boundless, timeless, ever reaching into the future so you have to put time frames around it and your decisions, and the Timeline Plan is a way of doing this.

With this relationship I did the following, and adapted it as things unfolded.

* Gave it a month to see if my feelings would change (more specifically if he suddenly saw the light about the joys of yoghurt).
* After a month I told him that I wanted to break up.
* After a week of him not accepting the break up, I called him to tell him to stop texting.
* After a week of him still texting, I blocked his number.
* After he contacted me on social media, I blocked him on there as well.

* After he turned up at my flat, I told him I would call the police and set the dogs on him if he came back again.

That last one did the trick and meant I didn't have to hire a pack of rabid dogs.

What the hell was going on? I mean, I'm not that much of a catch … (erm, that was your cue to go, 'Oh yes you are, James, you're *gorgeous* and handsome, like a statuesque Roman gladiator but with the dark brooding looks of Mr Darcy,' but whatever).

For the first time in ages, I was able to sleep properly without worrying about a phone call or a text or a direct message on social media trying to persuade me to change my mind. I could breathe again because I had placed time frames on my stress. The Timeline Plan was in action.

Basically, you need to look ahead, so it's saying things like:

* If my workload hasn't improved in a month, I'll speak to my boss.
* If my child's behaviour doesn't improve in two weeks, I'll speak to their teacher.
* If my bills are still too high in six months, I'll look at ways to economise.
* If I don't like my new job in three months, I'll start looking for something else.

*   If my leg is still hurting in five weeks, I'll go to the
doctor.

As each milestone passes you can take action or reflect,
create different timescales and allow for things to change
and you can move forward.

After a month you might find that your workload has
improved but you speak to your boss anyway to make sure
it's not overwhelming in the future. Or when you speak to
their teacher about your child, you create new time frames
to make sure that the decisions you agree on are put in
place.

Time frames make stress more manageable because
it doesn't feel endless. You feel there are stop gaps, end
points and actions to be taken. There is a boundary around
the horrific feelings, and you feel more in control.

The really crucial thing is to make your Timeline Plan
quite specific, so saying 'I'll give it a few weeks or so and
see if my left ear grows back by itself' won't cut it.

You've got to create an alert on your calendar, write
it down somewhere, stick it on the fridge – wherever you
can't avoid it because ignoring is snoring, people, it's just
delaying tactics.

12. Be more Gina

Have you ever walked past a nightclub and seen a muscly guy in a skin-tight top trying to start a fight with another muscly guy in a skin-tight top, and there's a woman trying to drag him away shouting at the top of her voice, 'Andy! Andy! Stop it! Seriously Andy. IT'S NOT WORTH IT!'?

Well, sometimes you have to say to yourself, 'It's not worth it!' about your stress.

Andy's girlfriend is called Gina. She's very wise. She knows that some things are just not worth stressing about.

Gina is brilliant. She has perspective. She knows that things change. She knows that as time passes stress can pass or lessen or fade.

Stress is not worth the physical impact it can have on your body, your memory, your mental health, your relationships, your sense of worth, your confidence, your sleep, your job satisfaction, your joy.

It's not worth getting hit in the head by some douchebag outside a nightclub.

It's not worth YOU.

Now, it's understandable to be like Andy – acting without thinking, not seeing the bigger picture, running around like a headless chicken. To be fair, I don't think a headless chicken could punch anybody (nor would it look good in a skin-tight top), but you know what I mean.

Essentially, to manage stress we need to be more Gina and less Andy.

A colleague I used to work with would drive me madder than I am already, and that's fairly (and proudly) significantly mad.

They wouldn't do their share of the work; they would just do what they wanted and that meant doing the nice jobs not the horrid ones that everyone hated but still needed doing. They wouldn't talk to anyone in the staff room, they just sat grumpily in their chair. Always arrived late and left early. They were always off sick on a Monday...

It was infuriating, unfair and completely unjust. They knew I hated them and I'm quite, quite, quite sure they hated me too. I suspect you've met people like this.

I was getting more and more stressed. I couldn't sleep. I would hate going into work. I would come home and complain about them to my husband, who was initially sympathetic, but then grew tired of me telling stories of what they'd done and how much I loathed them. It was taking over my life. When I did sleep, I would have dreams about shouting at them.

I also didn't feel particularly proud of how much I despised them. I thought somehow, I should be better than that. But I wasn't. I'm not good with injustice, it gets me really, really cross.

After complaining to my boss, trying to engage them in the work and varying between being friendly and sending them daggers across my desk, I'd had enough. Nothing I did made any difference and all that happened is my health and wellbeing got worse and worse.

A year or so afterwards, the person got another job, which solved the situation, but the stress had taken a huge toll on my health. I had also grown to hate the job which I had once loved so much. I left and got another job.

As I look back now, I realise, as Gina would say, it wasn't worth it. My stress achieved nothing – in fact it just made things worse and worse and worse. I ended up bitter and unhappy. My immune system had taken a battering and I kept getting colds and bugs, and I had to rethink my whole career.

I want you to think about your own stress. Is the worry worth you? Will it matter in a year, five years, ten years? What *will* matter in a years' time, or five years' time or ten years' time is your damaged health, your damaged

49

relationships, your damaged confidence, your damaged self-esteem.

Just as Gina knew that Andy hitting the other bloke outside the nightclub was never going to be worth it, I want you to know that your stress isn't worth it either.

What is worth something is YOU.

13. Change thingybob

I'm moving house, which is always near the top of the list
in those internet articles about the most stressful events
you can go through.

Now, I think this is mostly nonsense when you look at
all the other stressful things you can go through – divorce,
bereavement, unemployment, serious illness – but still,
it's not exactly a spa retreat in Bali on the relaxation
spectrum.

We've just sold our flat in Scotland, moved to Brighton
and are renting whilst we look for somewhere else to buy.
We find somewhere we love, near the sea, with a lovely
courtyard garden and not too far from the train station.
Easy. We put in an offer. But obviously it's not as simple as
that. Of course not.

Our bank decides it no longer wants to give us a mortgage because I'm not working and Patrick is employed in
Ireland and getting paid in Euros. We can't buy the flat we
love.

I phone the bank and explain our excellent credit score, and the fact that Patrick's income is actually more than we were earning jointly before. After United Nations-like discussions and bargaining, they finally agree.

We make an offer on the lovely flat and then they change their mind a week later and say no. I phone the thirteen-year-old estate agent who tells me the owners will wait until we get another mortgage – big relief. But then a week later we see it's back on the market.

At this point I want to tear all the hair out of my head, but I have none so instead I daydream about bringing down the bank through illegal trading, bankrupting the estate agents and shouting at the idiot MP who's just declared on TV that he wasn't having an affair, he'd just slipped on some low-sugar orange juice on the pub floor, fell into the lap of the young woman in the bar and his lips accidently met hers – this has nothing to do with the flat you understand. I just hate him.

I'm ranting about this to my friend Ed in a pub (with no orange juice on the floor). He's shaking his head at the right times and buying me more cheese and chive crisps, because generally they make me feel better, but I feel like I'll need a seven hundred kilo bag to improve things.

ED: You know about the three Cs right?

ME: The three what?

ED: The three Cs.

ME: Unless that stands for Cheese and Chive Crisps, I'm not interested.

ED: If I buy you any more crisps my kids won't get new shoes next month. No, it's a change thingybob.

ME: A change thingybob? You must stop watching those inspirational talks on YouTube.

ED: Shut up and listen for a moment. The three Cs are the questions you have to ask yourself to manage stress.

ME: Can I have more crisps? Can you get me some more crisps? Can I buy shares in the crisp company?

ED: No, you fluffy buffoon. These are the questions. Can you change it? Can someone else help you change it? Can you change the way you think about it?

ME: How does that get me a mortgage?

ED: If you'll stop stuffing your face for one minute I'll explain. Can you change the situation with the mortgage?

ME: I don't know, I could try and speak with them again I suppose?

ED: Great. Can someone else help change it?

ME: I suppose Patrick hasn't spoken to them yet, and I haven't been in touch with a mortgage broker to look at other alternatives.

ED: Going well, you big baldy crisp junkie. Now, can you change the way you think about it?

ME: Oh bugger off.

ED: I'm serious. Look into your heart and think if you can change the way you think about it.

ME: Bloody hell, that's what the inspirational talk guy said isn't it?

ED: He might have done, yes.

ME: Fine. Okay, fine. So, I suppose there might be other flats that come onto the market. When I find a job, it will be easier to get a mortgage and there's still some hope it might work out, I guess.

ED: Well done, you have now reached Theta Change Level seventy-four and can apply for eternal spiritual enlightenment.

ME: And more crisps?

ED: Yes, and more crisps.

These days, when I'm stressed about anything I use the three Cs. Remember, these are:

* Can you change it?
* Can someone else help you change it?
* Can you change the way you think about it?

It can be stressing over something small like the neighbours playing loud music on a Sunday morning or the
person at the front of the post office queue who has
seventy-four parcels and can't find their wallet, as it's
under all the parcels.

It can also be big stuff. Finance, relationships, family
issues or parenting – I only have a cat but I imagine if
you're a parent a large portion of stress comes from trying
to raise children to be good adults and not yoghurt-hating
sociopaths.

Try out the three C questions on your stress now. You
don't necessarily need to use all the questions, sometimes
one or two will work to move things forward.

You also need to examine each of the questions really
thoroughly, as we have a tendency when we're stressed to
react and dismiss possible solutions.

It can really help to go through them with someone else,
it doesn't need to be my friend Ed, although he says he's
available at very reasonable rates. Other people can bring
their own unique take on your situation, they can ask
questions and often have ideas that you haven't thought
about. They are able to take a broader and more objective
view of the situation because they're not living through it
themselves.

If all else fails, buy some cheese and chive crisps.

14. Children and lambs and all the lovely, lovely things

'We're going to see some lambs,' said my friend Helen. 'It will be good for you.'

'Lambs?' I said. 'I'm stressed and you're taking me to see lambs?! What are they going to do, give me a ninety-minute wool and rosemary aromatherapy session?

But off we went into the country, me moaning about the lack of wifi and being too far away from essentials like organic coffee shops and twenty-four-hour sushi delivery services.

We walked down a muddy lane, me still complaining, this time about my dirty shoes, the smell of manure and the lack of charger sockets that, in my opinion, should be built into every tree.

'Stop bloody whinging, we're just around the corner now,' said Helen, I suspect now doubting whether this was a good idea in the first place.

A minute later, we saw the lambs.

They were bouncing, they were running, they were playing, they were sleeping, they were snuggling up to their mums, they were all white and fluffy and completely lovely. There was an utter joy to them. A freedom. A complete purity that was instantly infectious.

'Look at them,' I said quietly, and Helen smiled.

I stared for about a minute. I'd seen lambs before, of course, but I hadn't seen them when I'd been this stressed. This was weird, the lambs were ... well, they were making me feel better. What kind of mint sorcery was this?

57

Then Helen led me to some stables where we saw a farmer helping children to feed bottles of milk to some other lambs. For goodness sake, what was this waterfall of innocence?

The lambs guzzled the milk whilst the children held them. It was difficult to see who was having the better time. The children giggled and grinned, the parents smiled, the lambs wiggled their tails and, in all honesty, at this point I was expecting a choir of angels in gold embroidered robes to start singing *All Things Bright and Beautiful* in D major with God accompanying them on a double row tambourine.

Helen stared at me with an 'I told you so' look on her face as I started to cry.

Part of me was thinking, 'Get a bloody grip, James, it's just lambs and children,' but whenever thoughts like

this come, it's really, really, *really* important that you tell
them to bugger off. So, instead of being cynical and telling
myself to get a grip, I just let the tears flow and enjoyed
the sight of lambs and children and the utter delight of
it all.

We went for lunch where we decided against the lamb
chops and Helen told me that this was one of the ways
she deals with her own stress – by seeking out innocence
wherever she can. Finding things that are untouched by
cynicism and doubt – by which, I assume, she meant me.

When we connect to innocent things like lambs and
children, it has a profound impact on us when we're
stressed.

Now, some science person would be able to tell you
about what the brain does when you see lovely things;
probably some neurons and receptors combining to ... no,
I've actually no idea. The good thing is we don't need to
understand all the neurological complexities. It makes you
feel better, which is what counts.

You don't need to head out into the country at spring-
time when the lambs are frolicking around. You can go to
a zoo and find a sloth, or smile at the children pretending
to be aeroplanes in a park, or head round to your friend's
house and cuddle their cat. I have been known to phone up
my friend and insist I need to come round on some pretext
like 'checking the consistency of the grout between their

bathroom tiles', when in fact all I wanted was to spend a good half an hour cuddling and playing with their dogs.

What matters is Observing Innocence (which is also the title of my nine-part Nordic crime drama). Seek it out when the world is pressing down on you, and it will pay you back.

59

15. Oi, do me a favour

The thing with stress is that it feels impossibly heavy.

It's like you're dragging around sixteen large pissed-off African bush elephants on your back. You have to lighten the load.

The daily ups and downs of life are hard enough. Nagging someone to unload the dishwasher. Remembering to buy toilet roll. Trying to get three children to three separate after-school clubs on the same evening at opposite ends of the town. Buying a present for your great nephew who only reads obscure imported manga comics in their original Japanese. Trying to find time to call your mother-in-law to explain what the internet is and how it doesn't plant a microchip into your head and read your mind. When you add in other, more serious stresses, things become unmanageable and the elephants get heavier and heavier.

You have to get help with the smaller stressors to manage the bigger ones – our nervous systems are not made to deal with seven hundred things at one time.

Call in favours from other people – friends, relatives, anyone who can assist in the short term to make things lighter. To do this **YOU HAVE TO ASK.**

Pride be damned because, firstly, there's no shame in saying you need some help; we all do at some point and anyone who says different is a plonker and lying. Secondly, people like to help. They really do. It makes them feel useful and it's a demonstrable way for them to show how much they love you. Thirdly, you will repay the favour when they need help, so it all evens out over time.

If people say, 'How can I help?', the trick is not to go, 'Help? Me! Nooooo. I don't need any help. I'm totally fine, completely and utterly okay. All okey dokey in my world thanks. Sure, I was swallowed by a blue whale, digested in their stomach for three months, then spat out again and had to swim seventeen miles to shore but NOOO, I don't need your help. What a ridiculous notion. What's that? There's something in my hair? Oh yes, it's fine, that's just a bit of mucus from the whale's third stomach chamber.'

Ask if someone can take the kids to the park for a few hours, or perhaps a friend can cook a few meals, so you don't need to think about food for a few nights. Ask a colleague to walk the dog – if you don't have a dog, then that's just a silly thing to ask. See if someone can come round and do a few loads of washing, or give the lounge a vacuum,

61

or change the bed sheets, or clean the fridge, or be there
when the shopping delivery arrives and pack it all away, or
buy some flowers for the woman next door who has flu.

There's a reason why people bring round food when
you've experienced a bereavement or when you've moved
house; it's because there is so much else going on that
you don't have the time or the desire to cook something
healthy from scratch when the removal men have taken all
the garden furniture to the bathroom and you need to plan
a funeral for your aunt who specified in her will that her
thirty-five cats must be in attendance.

I've learnt the hard way that stoicism, reticence and
a ridiculous sense of self-reliance get you nowhere when
managing stress. Please, please let people help you. Things
that I do now when my stress is high include:

* Asking people to weed my garden
* Asking people to pick up milk and other essentials
  when I've forgotten them
* Asking people to water my houseplants when I'm
  away
* Asking people to iron my work clothes
* Asking people to help me fix the fridge, boiler, oven,
  washing machine, etc.
* Asking people to buy me yoghurt
* Asking people to feed the cat

* Asking people to vacuum for me
* Asking people to make me some packed lunches for work
* Asking people to clean my windows

When I'm struggling with my stress I think about the smaller, practical things that people can help with that will make it easier for me. I ask people that won't mind, that want to help and that, crucially, won't judge the state of my bathroom cabinet.

63

16. Structure, so you don't rupture

I'm chatting with my therapist.

I say chatting; what's really happening is I'm offloading all my stuff like a lorry spilling its load on the M25.

> ME: And then I had to go round and tell him that it was all unacceptable because, you know, it's just not okay, is it? I'm so stressed about what he said to me, so, I had go over there, talk to him, but I forgot to feed the cat, so I had to come back early, feed the cat and then go back again – then afterwards I had to get some shopping in but by the time I got to the supermarket it had run out of the nice toilet roll, so I had to get a bus to another shop that did have the nice toilet rolls – you know, the quilted ones that are just that bit softer – then I forgot my keys, so I had to go round to my friend's house to get the spare key, but they were out so I had to sleep at my other friend's house, and by the time I got home the next day the cat had been sick

on the carpet and the washing machine had flooded,
so I didn't have lunch, then I had to go back and talk
to him because I realised there was more I needed to
say and then go to the shop where I got the washing
machine because their website had broken, but this
was after work so they were shut and so I took a day
off work but I didn't sleep the night before and went on
the Wednesday when they were open, but they were
actually shut so I got my sister to feed the cat, took a
day off work and went on Thursday instead.

THERAPIST: Right.

ME: Terrible, eh?

THERAPIST: I'm just wondering . . . its just all sounds
very . . . busy. Where's your stability, your routine, your
structure to keep you safe, in all of this?

She had a point.

You see, stress is the big disruptor, it buggers
everything up. It's like you've just completed a one-
thousand-piece jigsaw and then an over-exuberant puppy
comes bouncing in and trashes it all.

When stress hits, you need a structure to hold you,
to keep you focused and in check. Routine is one way of
doing this. It's like stabilisers when you first started to
ride a bike. Amidst the scariness there needs to be
safety.

When stress is flying at me like the birds in the Hitchcock film, I don't feed the chaos (or the birds). I stick to my routine even more than I would do normally.

I eat at the same time each day. Breakfast at eight o'clock. Lunch at twelve-thirty. Dinner at half seven.

I also stick to my regular foods and don't introduce new things, like cajun and Carolina reaper chilli pepper tofu bites, into my diet. My stomach can then have a bit of peace and doesn't go, 'Woah there, mister, what the hell was *that*?' The link between stress and stomach issues is well-documented, so we have to watch what goes in the latter. Be friends to your tummy whilst your stressed, it will really appreciate it.

You might watch your favourite soap opera at the same time each week, in which case stick to it, keep that date with your character who has returned from the dead as his evil twin's ex-lover for the third time. It's important, and I don't mean that flippantly.

Television is great because it has a regular schedule, but I do this for on-demand TV as well. When I'm stressed, I'll plan my television week and make sure that on a Wednesday, at the same time each week, I'll watch 'undemanding trash' – which is a new sub-genre I've invented and works brilliantly with stress.

You can shower at the same time each morning. Do that word puzzle on your phone at lunchtime each day. Water the garden before you go to bed. Anything that marks the day as similar to others.

Unlike me – rushing around on buses trying to find the right toilet roll and having to stay at my friend's house – when you're stressed you should plan your time carefully to ensure you build in routine and structure.

Routine is the poles when the wind is threatening to blow your tent down.

67

17. Boxes with hairs (yes, that is the title of this chapter)

We're going to do some drawing. Fear not, we won't enter your picture into your local art society's annual gala. It's just a way of planning what to do about your stress in the short and long term.

Yes, I could have called the hairs 'threads' instead, but this way it's more fun and it gives me a thrill because I don't have any hair.

This is a kind of 'draw along with James' thing, so you'll need some paper (it's the stuff that we used before computers). You can use your computer too though.

What we do is we draw a box, like this:

Please draw your box too.

Inside the box we're going to write down one thing that is causing us stress. It has to be one thing at a time I'm afraid, as otherwise it all gets too complicated. You can draw more boxes obviously, but they need to contain just one stressor each.

I'm going to give you an example of planning my wedding, which was SO stressful. I mostly did it myself because my beloved boyfriend (at the time) claimed his skills lay best in 'idea generation' – which amounted to suggesting we buy lots of champagne. I mean, that's a great suggestion and everything, but it doesn't actually help with the sourcing and buying of it, nor did it help with planning the rest of the frigging wedding.

69

Here we go.

You write the stressor in the box like this. I encourage swearing by the way.

Next you are going to add short hairs coming out of the
box for short-term action and think about what this might
include.

Here was mine.

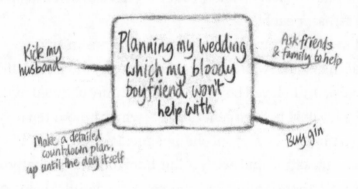

Then you add in the longer hairs for long-term action, in
my case on the wedding day itself.

You end up with the box looking like this with short hairs for the short-term action and long hairs for the long-term action.

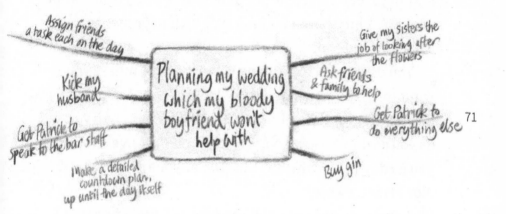

You can have as many hairs as you want; you could do a really detailed box and make it look like a highland cow or just keep it to a few. The trick is to have enough hairs so that you feel some sense of control over your stress.

When I see people white water rafting, paddling furiously with someone shouting commands to steer this way or move to the right a bit, I think, well what's the point? You're all being shunted down a raging torrent at high speed, with thousands of tonnes of water flowing over death defying rocks and you're attempting to steer? What's the point?

But the leader knows what needs to be done at the start

of the river and what needs to be done at the end. He has a plan if someone goes into the water, and he knows how to manoeuvre the raft so it doesn't hit the nasty rocks making everyone topple out. It feels like everything is out of control, but the leader has made a plan for the start and a plan for the end.

You don't need to go white water rafting, unless you want to, it's just a useful way of looking at it. But hey, if you do go white water rafting you could draw your hairy boxes as you go down. How cool would that be? Or live *stream* as you go down. Stream. Stream? Did anyone get that joke? No? I'll get my coat.

You can spend some time on your box too. I find that I have some immediate ideas and then if I leave it a while, and as life carries on, other ideas spring to mind. It's a sort of evolving thing, the hairs grow and develop over time (unlike on my head). You might find one doesn't work so you give it a trim and others work well so you carry on with those.

18. Getting away, not running away

I've gone to Montenegro, as you do.

I had to get away. I'm getting frustrated at work and want to shout at everyone. I'm recovering from a virus which has left me so out of breath I can't even look at people jogging without being exhausted, and the daily news is so unbelievably dreadful I can't watch it, but then feel bad for not watching it, if that make sense.

On a whim I book a flight and an apartment overlooking the water, and head off. It's not the most well thought out thing I've ever done. I haven't looked to see what language I need to speak or what the currency is, but hey, everywhere takes cards now, right? (Wrong – top tip: take cash to Montenegro).

I sit on my balcony watching the swifts bounce around excitedly over the sea, experiencing the glorious sound of the cathedral bells every hour and seeing the sun setting over the mountains each evening. I manage to breathe a little.

I take a couple of day trips to Albania and Bosnia. I buy cheese and honey from a farmer's market and Patrick some hand-knitted socks from an older woman who tells me they are 'warm enough to milk the cows in wintertime'. I don't think Patrick comes across any cows in our back garden that need milking in December, but it's always best to be prepared.

I wander through old Montenegrin towns, across shiny marble pavements, and feed stray cats with treats I've brought from home. They're fearful, but once I get down to their level and put the little tuna-flavoured biscuits on the floor they hang around, still looking behind them in case of attack, but grateful; well, as grateful as cats ever are. More of a quick, nonchalant 'yeah, cheers, thanks a lot mate' kind of a backwards glance when they finish eating. Then they're quickly absorbed back into the medieval alleyways.

I see different things each day. New beaches, different birds. Some fantastic, belligerent Montenegrin goats who take up the whole road because munching roadside hedges is much more important than alleviating traffic jams.

There are quiet back-street churches sunk in history and hope. Different food being sold in different supermarkets. I buy what I think is orange juice, but it turns out to be some sort of delicious pomegranate and apricot blend which I then buy every day to have with breakfast.

I take a boat into the bay with scenery so beguiling it feels unreal. I get off at a church set on an island and wonder at the commitment it would take to go each Sunday if that was your nearest place of worship.

I find a town with red geraniums on shuttered balconies. Restaurants by the water and pastel ice-cream stands. I sit and watch the rowing boats happily being bounced on the waves like a new grandchild on a proud granny's lap.

Each evening I cook too much pasta, pour some local wine and watch the sunset over the bay before heading to bed. I don't watch television. I don't check social media. I don't check the news. It's a real break.

Being somewhere unfamiliar and beautiful has let the stress fade. I haven't forgotten about it all, it's not going to completely solve it and there are times when it all pops into my head, but physically removing myself from my usual surroundings for a while is helping.

Creating some physical distance from home, where my stress lives, gives me perspective. It's freed up my mind to tackle the stress, develop a plan of action, given me some room to breathe. I've had time and space to let the stress settle. I understand it more and know what to do next. Just as we take time off when we're ill to recuperate, we need to do the same with stress.

At home it felt like being in a maze trapped with crowds

and crowds of people shouting, unable to move or see or hear. Now, I'm still in the maze but I can start to find a way out, even if it may take a little while and I might need to raise a white flag and get someone to help me out – but that's okay, and I can practise (and keep practising) all that I've learnt when I was away, now that I'm back home.

You can't always head off to Montenegro on a whim, obviously, especially if you have five children and a cow to milk, so it's worth thinking about alternatives.

Sometimes a day trip to somewhere new will be enough, or a stay with a friend in another part of the country (being clear with them that you might need some time to yourself), or a cheap-ish bed and breakfast a train ride away.

It takes a bit of investment of time and money, but the rewards are seeing a clearer path.

19. Look after your body, bro

I'm at my doctors' surgery, again. I've been so often
recently I'm seriously considering asking them to convert
the upper floor into a penthouse for my personal use.

DOCTOR: How are you?

ME: Well, my eye has been twitching so much recently
and my heart feels like it's beating really fast and my
stomach feels terrible, churning and painful and I have
this terrible headache all the time. I'm fine really.

DOCTOR: Is there any stress in your life?

ME: No, I don't think so. Well, a big bereavement, I've
been unemployed for a year now. Lots of family arguments. I relocated a few months ago. I'm on benefits so
I haven't got much money and my husband is working
abroad.

DOCTOR: That's a huge amount. How are you looking
after yourself?

ME: Sorry?

DOCTOR: How are you looking after your body? We'll do some blood tests but some of these symptoms sound like stress. Can I check a few things?

ME: Sure.

DOCTOR: Are you eating properly? Are you sleeping? Are you drinking enough? Are you getting any exercise?

ME: Oh, well . . . I don't tend to eat much during the day, I just don't feel very hungry really – sometimes I'll have an evening meal, usually a packet of crisps. I do drink coffee, mostly espressos, to stay hydrated. I'm not sleeping much – I feel too wired and I haven't joined a gym because I can't afford it and when I go for a walk I just think about all the things that have gone wrong and so I tend to stay indoors.

DOCTOR: Right. Just so I've got this clear. You're barely eating, you're drinking too much caffeine and getting dehydrated, your sleeping is deeply problematic, you're not exercising and you're not going outside?

ME: I guess. Okay, yes, when you put it like that, I see your point. I'll do better, I promise. [*I look around the room*] Have you thought about making this into a penthouse?

Now, I'm not one of those ridiculous people who insists that the cure for stress is swimming thirteen miles in your local village pond before five am, drinking mineral water exclusively from Alsace-Lorraine and juicing seventeen Peruvian groundcherries for lunch.

Actually, I don't even have a juicer anymore because I was only making cocktails and *apparently* it's not good for you to have triple-strength absinthe mojitos before breakfast. Who knew?

But still, the doctor had a point. Stress impacts the body, and you have to look after your body to manage stress – the two go together. This means doing all the things that your mum said were important when you were eight. You have to parent yourself to manage your stress.

I'm no doctor, as you can probably tell, so any worries you have, get an appointment with one, but I can tell you what works for me.

When I'm stressed, I don't want to eat anything but for some people it's the opposite and they want to eat more. Balance is key, so getting my daily fruit and veg is important. I don't overload on sugar, which just gives me a big rush but then dumps me on the floor like a discarded cigarette butt outside a dodgy pub near the railway station.

Some comfort food is obviously okay, but I eat regular meals now, not just a packet of crisps. My body needs fuel, and my brain needs feeding to manage what's happening to me.

Similarly, I have to hydrate. Water, water, water! Not

just espresso shots. It all helps with the whole keeping your body going thing.

Sleep is *so* important people. Stress can massively disrupt it and my body needs it to restore and face the stress. When I don't sleep everything seems worse in the morning. It causes me to doze off in the afternoon because I haven't slept and then I can't sleep again at night and it all gets buggered up in a hideous cycle of waking up at three o'clock in the morning, wondering where everything went wrong and staring in the bathroom mirror wondering whether my face looks like a lopsided parsnip.

When it comes to exercise, there's no need to sign up for the local marathon (I mean you can if you want, but it's not essential for managing stress, thank goodness). I cycle – I love the feeling of getting from place to place fairly quickly under my own steam – but brisk walking also works. The key for me is sweating a bit, getting my heart rate up.

I suspect the exercise experts would say 'do something you love', which is good advice, but I would say 'do something you love and are able to do'.

As much as I love volleyball, I'm truly terrible at it. I saw it live at the Olympics and thought, 'Yeah, I could do that, bit of jumping, bit of hitting over the net, seems easy enough.' Oh, sweet reader, I am not a natural volleyballer.

The ball itself is like really, really hard. I went to hit it over the net and hit it under instead, which isn't allowed or something – ridiculous rule if you ask me. This is why I cycle, because I love it *and* I'm able to do it; the lack of a net is also advantageous.

Your body is the vessel that's carrying around your stress. You might feel it in your neck or shoulders or stomach, and all those parts need looking after carefully. If you want the water to stay in your glass you carry it carefully. What I was doing was shaking the glass all over the place and expecting the water to settle down. I'm no physics buff but I can tell you it just doesn't work like that.

When you're experiencing stress look after your body because it will help you to manage the stress.

81

20. Distraction   Sorry, what did you say again?

I'm going away for the weekend, and I've hurt my back. These things always happen at the most inconvenient times, don't they?

I've agreed to climb a mountain.

Generally, I'm quite happy at sea level and have no interest in climbing anything other than an escalator to a cocktail bar but it's for a great charity that I support.

The organisers reassure me it's worth the view and I've already got sponsorship money in from friends and family, who have sent me messages like, 'You can do it, James, you old bugger!' and 'Climb that damn mountain you prick!' Charming.

I'm worried that climbing – well walking very, very slowly – up a mountain is going to make my back worse, but now we're on a minibus to Wales, someone is handing out Kendal Mint Cake and I seem to be the only one who doesn't regularly spend their weekends jogging up to

Mount Everest-like altitudes. 'Oh yes, we been up this one before,' says a man twice my age. 'I'm hoping to beat my best time.' I'm sorry, are we in some kind of race now?

I've bought some new walking boots that are already rubbing on my heels as we start off. Quickly it becomes apparent that: a) I'm not a mountain goat; and b) my back still really hurts. Someone tries to get everyone singing 'One Man Went to Mow', and I just about resist the temptation to throw them over the side into the ravine.

83

An hour passes and we stop for lunch, each of us perched on a rock eating our sandwiches before a magnificent view of fields and a silver river snaking its way to the coast. I get talking to a woman who tells me about a dog she adopted, and I tell her about my ridiculous cat who adopted us, and then we set off again.

Three hours later we're at the top. It's a bit misty so it's not quite the magical experience they promised, but it feels like a huge achievement. I add a rock to a pile of other rocks, which is apparently the thing to do and then I realise that I haven't noticed the pain in my back until now. I can vaguely remember it twinging a little, but it wasn't on my mind all the time as it had been in the preceding days. I'm genuinely surprised. I realise I didn't notice it because there was so much else going on; mainly trying not to fall to my death halfway up a mountain.

This, folks, is the power of distraction. It's a great tool to have at hand when you're experiencing stress.

You'll be glad to know you don't need to find a handy hill to crawl up when you need it – loads of other things work.

My husband makes lists, mainly of films that he's watched. He categorises them and then ranks them. I play word games on my phone or find some really, really trashy television that makes my brain cells disappear as I'm watching it. Try reading, listening to music or podcasts. Basically, if you feel guilty for not doing the housework then it's probably the right activity. Oh, and housework can help too.

It's about getting a break from your stress. Finding time so you're not constantly thinking about it. But just to be really clear, distraction is not denial.

I'm not suggesting you do other things to ignore your stress, this isn't a bury your head in the sand kind of thing; that won't work, and you'll just get sand in your hair. Distraction doesn't take the stress away; it helps you to take a break so that you can re-group and manage it better.

I'll be honest, I haven't been up a mountain since. The walking boots remain in the shed covered in mud, but the charity got a few quid from me and I learned the importance of distraction that day, and that was invaluable.

21. I'm at my limit

I'm having one of those weeks where it's all got too much.

I have to sort out my house insurance, pet insurance and travel insurance. I have to get a quote to replace the windows, prune the tree in the garden and my husband is seriously ill with a genetic condition. Work is ridiculously busy and the cat has decided to start bringing in small black mice to hide in my shoes. I can't really cope with much more but then, of course, the ceiling collapses in the bedroom.

I sit in the garden, underneath the overgrown tree, and cry. I'd had enough. At this point I wouldn't have been surprised if the tree fell on me and, frankly, it would be something of a relief – but a shame for the nice tree.

The amount of stress is unsustainable. I phone my cousin Nick, who's wise beyond his years and is always a steadying counterpoint to my often somewhat over emotional state.

Thankfully he answers and after a few minutes of him

trying to understand what I'm saying between the tears, he says, 'Something has got to give James, because other- wise you will.' I stop crying for a few seconds and realise how right he is. 'You've hit rock bottom, which I think is good, you have to break down to break through. You need to place limits on things James, put boundaries in place to manage all of this.'

We talk about how I can make things easier, how extremely stressed minds can't sort out stress, so you have to take things away to see what you need to do.

'A tree under attack from a disease can't breathe if it's being strangled by weed,' says Nick. I forgive him for all these phrases that sound as though they've come from an inspirational quotes Instagram account, the kind that has a sunset background to them – because they're often true, which is really, really annoying.

I realise that I can't support others at the moment so I cut back on the charity work I'm doing – I would only cover people in snot, which seems unfair. I speak to work and ask if I can cut back on extra jobs I've taken on. I get people to help with doing the mundane things I can't face at the moment – all the insurance stuff and the tree.

I say no to going to a party of a friend of a friend which is causing me more stress because it's an *Alice in Wonderland*-themed fancy dress and funnily enough I don't have a spare white rabbit costume. Taking my cat, renaming him 'Cheshire' and asking him to grin for the evening won't really cut it. I don't answer the phone to my friend who only talks about their own problems, never asks me about how I am and leeches every sap of energy from me.

With all these things taken off my plate I'm able to focus on my husband and his illness. We get a second opinion from a doctor and he's put on different medication, which seems to stabilise things.

I've seen far too many people burn out because of the amount of stress that they're juggling. Let's say it again: it's not sustainable, something will snap.

Imagine a twig. One you see on the floor in the woods whilst walking in the countryside. I want you to pick it up. It's one of those green ones that you can twist and turn, not one of the dry ones that just snaps. Hold it in your hands. Get the feel of it.

Now, I want you to start twisting it. Twist it once. Twist it again, and again – it's still intact but has come apart a bit. Keep twisting and twisting and twisting. More of it comes apart and eventually the whole things breaks in two.

When the twig breaks we can patch it up, and it still looks like a twig but it is more susceptible to breaks than before. So, it always better to manage things as you go along. Don't take on too much. Keep things on a more balanced keel.

Now, admittedly, you're not a twig, but this is what happens when we have more and more and more stress and don't do anything about it.

We break.

I've broken on numerous occasions in the past because I didn't tackle my stress. I've carried on and ignored the signs – insomnia, lack of appetite, panic attacks, anxiety and low mood. I didn't admit how difficult things were and I didn't do anything to rectify it.

I've carried on in jobs that made me ill, I've carried on with relationships that made me ill, I've continued friendships that made me ill. I've been so ill that I ended up in a psychiatric hospital, on anti-depressants and sleep medication. Now, that's an extreme outcome but not out of the realms of possibility for any of us.

I really, really don't want you to get to that point because psychiatric hospitals these days don't have hot spring jacuzzis, mountain views, personal butler service, wood-fired saunas, hot stone massage sessions and room service. Standards have really slipped, eh?

Extremes are really bad with stress.

For example, before talking with Nick I was tempted to resign from my job and have done with everything so I could just look after my husband but that would have been foolish as I needed the money, the break and the dis-traction. Plus being in the house at the same time all day together would have ended badly, and yellow crime tape doesn't go with the green sofa.

Know your limits.

Know them before the stick breaks.

Know that you have to reduce other things to stay on the right path and ensure that the stick does not snap.

22. Livin' la Vida Lois

I want you to imagine you're a limpet called Lois, living in Puertito de Los Molinos, Fuerteventura. You didn't think you'd be reading that sentence when you got up this morning, now did you?

Lois is gripping to her rock and ain't nobody gonna get her off. Not that pesky seagull flying overhead. Not that kid with a spade. No ma'am, ain't nobody moving her. She's clinging on to what she knows, because the waves are getting choppy.

When we're stressed, we need dependable objects, people and experiences to cling on to.

It's like ballet dancers who pick a spot whilst they're spinning to stop them from falling over. Or when you've had too much to drink and need to hold onto the bar – I've seen you after a couple of tequila shots.

Stability is essential when the world is turning upside down. If Dorothy in *The Wizard of Oz* had just held onto her house that little bit more, she wouldn't have got into such a mess.

For Lois, the rock in her life is . . . well, it's her rock, but the rest of us need to find other things to help our stability when things are stressful.

Old friends who know you well come into their own. The ones that don't judge you because of your obsession with Irrawaddy Dolphins. The ones you can phone at four o'clock in the morning. The ones who didn't pass judgement on your denim-on-denim fashion phase when you were fifteen.

It's important to spend time with them. You can talk about your stress if you want, or don't talk about it at all and just go to your favourite café for a latte and a gossip or sit in their garden and look at the flowers. What's important is their steadying presence. Connect with the friends who are your ballast.

I often re-read much loved books or watch my favourite sitcoms or films when I'm stressed. There's comfort in familiarity. I don't need to concentrate too much; I know what's going to happen so there are no sudden shocks; I can be with fictional people who I know and love. Stress makes us fearful of what's going to happen in the future so being in a world where you know it all turns out okay, really helps.

I go on cycle rides that I love, where I know the pathway and there aren't any huge surprise mammoth hills in my way – just lovely views. I know the terrain, I know how

long it will take and I know that I can get home easily.
It's familiar and reassuring and I don't need to think too
much.

I go back to treasured second-hand bookshops and
rummage around. I take in the intoxicating aroma of old
paper and polished wood, and flick through books that
have been read by many hands. I feel a sense of connection
and stability.

I stock up on comfort food that I love, often from
childhood. I'll buy a Swiss roll or a banana milkshake or
a packet of mints – all the healthy stuff as you can see. Or
I'll cook my great grandmother's kedgeree recipe, handed
down through the generations.

93

I change the bed linen to my favourite duvet cover and
sheets. I'll get my blanket which I've had for years (I'm
not actually sure it's ever been washed but anyway) and
cuddle up in bed.

There's a reason why children bring a teddy bear or soft
toy out with them – they need security in a strange world
that's hard to understand. It's the same for us when we're
stressed, we need familiar, soothing things with us – and
yes, I give you permission to carry around a cuddly giraffe
if you want.

23. Give me joy in my meaningful mung bean salad

I know at the moment you don't think you can experience any joy in your life because everything is crap.

Stress leeches out all the joy of life, so you have to bring it back in to balance things out. Stress pushes the scales in the direction of hopelessness and joy will help even this out.

Joy is not the same as happiness. They're like second cousins, maybe they share a few genes, but they're very different.

What we're talking about here are feeling moments of **JOY**.

There's more nourishment in joy than happiness. It's the difference between eating a sleazy burger covered in processed cheese from a dodgy stand outside a night-club, compared to one of those salads with mung beans, avocado, pomegranate seeds, organic spinach leaves and kohlrabi – no, I don't know what kohlrabi is either, but I'm sure it's good for you.

I want you to look back at old photos on your phone or on social media or in photograph albums or in your memory bank and find the holidays, parties, birthdays, day trips, times when you laughed with a friend – anything when you had a piercing, overwhelming feeling of joy.

The times when stress was pushed aside and you just felt a momentous shift in your mood, where everything was not just okay, but heavenly, a blissful beam of loveliness took you over completely, however briefly.

These memories counteract the stress. They're proof that things change, that you'll laugh uncontrollably when seeing your friend trying to eat spaghetti with a teaspoon. That you will be amazed by a sunset at the beach, spilling red beauty into the sea. That you will grin at the dog rolling on his back with glee in the grass.

When I'm stressed, I think about the time in a supermarket queue when ABBA's 'Dancing Queen' was playing on the radio and everyone waiting started to dance.

I think about being on the beach with my friend and suddenly an avalanche of bubbles came billowing around us from a child's toy.

I think about being in a butterfly farm surrounded by colour and beauty at every turn.

I think about being under a cherry tree and the wind suddenly whipping up and blowing the petals all around me like a stunning confetti tornado.

95

I think about stroking Icelandic ponies in the snow by the sea – okay they bit a member of the group, but for me it was wonderful.

I'm fed by these memories; they remind me that I'm not my stress. They nudge my current problems out of the way and point me toward joyful times in the past, which in turn shows me that my current life can have joy in it and that, absolutely crucially, my future can be joyous again too.

Alongside joy, I try and get as much meaningful stuff as I can into my life. Joy on one side, meaningful stuff on the other. The two go together perfectly to manage stress.

What I mean by this is activities that have depth and sustain you – again like a mung bean salad. Getting drunk in your bedroom might seem like a great stress-relieving activity, but it won't help carry you through the difficult periods in your life.

When you find something meaningful, which is greater than your stress, your stress will start to recede.

For me, I sink into a novel. Usually historical crime these days as I love the problem-solving and the sense of the past enveloping me. I never come away from reading my book and think, 'Well, that was a waste of time.' I always feel like my brain has had a good workout, that I've thought about things in a different way or been given a different perspective on the world.

I also try and grow stuff in the garden. I have a strict rule that I'll only plant things that won't die and won't get eaten by slugs. This narrows down the field a little, but it does make the experience much more enjoyable when you don't wake up to a family of slugs sitting down to brunch on the expensive hostas you've just bought from the garden centre. Yes, it still hurts. No, I'm not over it.

It could be that hiking is your thing. Or stock car racing. Or watching your football team lose every Saturday or umpiring the junior hockey match or contributing to a community patchwork quilt or making a great salad for when your friends come over ...

I've volunteered in the past – giving back is a great way to manage your own stress. You feel connected to others and connected to your community. Run a jumble sale for charity, volunteer at the local dog shelter, pick up litter from a beauty spot, or just come and feed my cat. Volunteering helps you feel that you're contributing to the world, making other people's lives better and improving your own in turn.

Remember, with joy and with meaningful activity, think mung bean salad not sleazy burger.

24. Be less snail – connect don't disconnect

When we're stressed, we turn into snails. Trust me, this will make sense, I promise.

When snails are under attack, they tuck their heads into their shells for protection. They withdraw to avoid being hurt or eaten, and we tend to do the same. We don't actually have a shell ourselves and it's not often we have to worry about being eaten by a bird, but you get my drift.

We retreat. We disconnect from our loved ones. We shy away from spending time with people because we worry we'll be judged. We don't go for that weekend drink in the pub because it all feels like too much effort when you're only just getting through the day. We feel ashamed that we're 'not managing' and think we'll be burdening others. We go into our shell and try and survive as best we can.

The trouble with this is that our stress gets stuck inside us. It has no outlet. It just spins around like a whirling dervish with nowhere to go and makes things worse.

Then we feel isolated because we're not seeing anyone. We feel that our stress has taken us over, there's no one to support us, no one to give us advice or provide a different perspective or let us talk – and talking is essential to manage your stress.

Stress needs an outlet and, because we humans are social creatures, we need to be with other humans who we like and value. It's a whole tribal thingy thing which I won't go into because firstly, I don't have a PhD in social anthropology and secondly, I don't understand it but anyway, it's true.

You have to do the opposite of what your stress is telling you to do, which is probably to stay under your duvet with seventeen pain au chocolats. Very tempting obviously, but solves nothing. It makes things worse in the long run and gets chocolate on your bed sheets.

Looking back on my times of stress, I always regret not reaching out for more support. Regrets are only useful when you make changes in the present. So, now I always remind myself about the importance of reaching out to get some help.

If you can afford some private counselling, then that can really help. The free stuff you'll probably have to wait a while for, but some counsellors offer low-cost options.

An objective, empathetic person who's just there for you can do wonders to help you see the path ahead. Just make sure you meet up with them first to see if you like them and check they're qualified. It's fine to have a few sessions and decide they're not the right person for you; counsellors are used to that. You need a good fit, someone that you feel comfortable and safe with, and maybe challenges you a bit too – in a nice way.

Friends and family can be just as useful to talk to, but remember they know you; they always want the best for you but won't always give you the best advice. If you just want to offload then say that at the start of the conversation, which might avoid your second cousin telling you the absolute best thing for stress is making dried artichoke hearts into earrings.

The act of talking is a weird one in many ways, it's amazing that it makes you feel better, but it does, and it's especially important to remember this when you don't want to talk to anyone.

The number of times when I've been stressed and thought 'I wish I hadn't arranged to see them for lunch,' and then I force myself to go and meet my friend and come away feeling better. Unburdened. Lighter. My stress has shrunk.

Similarly, I tend to avoid phone calls as they just feel like so much work but, when I speak to family and friends on the phone when I'm stressed, I end up feeling better because I've connected.

Now, I would avoid speaking to colleagues or friends of friends, who you don't know very well, because sometimes people say the wrong things or come out with some weird stuff that makes you just think, 'What on earth are they talking about?'

Or they immediately change the conversation to how stressed *they* are with their pet rats keeping them up at night, the affair they're having with a minor politician and how they can't get that red wine stain out of the hall carpet despite using bicarbonate of soda and everything. You'll come away thinking that making yourself vulnerable wasn't worth it and feeling exposed.

Find the right people to talk to, remember that talking helps and don't become a snail.

25. Just bloody well RELAX, okay?

'You just have to relax,' said my colleague once when I told them how stressed I was. 'Just calm down and relax.'

I don't know about you, but whenever someone tells me to 'just calm down and relax', I instantly want to smear their face in weasel poo. It *never* makes me feel relaxed and I get cross because I have no weasel poo to hand.

When managing stress, soothing is more important and much more realistic than trying to instantly be relaxed because someone has told you to be.

Just because a friend has paid for a private jet to take you to the Maldives, rented a private ocean view cabin, sprayed your bed sheets with a mixture of camomile tea and Valium and hired dolphins to sing lullabies to you each evening, doesn't mean your stress instantly goes away – but all these things will help soothe you.

However, I'm guessing you probably don't have a friend to take you to the Maldives on a private jet. No? Me neither, and I'm not entirely sure how soothing dolphin lullabies would be anyway; I suspect it would sound a bit too clicky. Let's look at other ways that don't involve the need to sell your kidney to raise the funds to go to a tropical island.

You could spend thousands of pounds on courses telling you how to practise breathing to soothe and ground you. I once did a six-month course on mindfulness, meditation and relaxing breathing, and learned nothing at all – none of the exercises helped.

103

Then I read a book which told me the best thing to do was sit still, breathe in for four seconds through my nose and then out for six through my mouth. That was it. So, that's all I do now. I don't gaze at a plastic lotus flower and go 'ommm', I don't visualise stroking a rainbow unicorn, I don't imagine I'm floating on a mattress of peace in the South China Sea.

I do that breathing technique a couple of times a day, more if I'm really stressed, and it makes me feel more grounded, more in the present. It doesn't remove the stress; it just gets my mind and body in a better state to tackle it.

It's pretty easy to remember: four and six. In for four, out slowly for six. Try it now. No, I mean actually try it, don't just read that sentence and not bother. I'll know if you haven't – I have spies everywhere. You can have a slice of coffee and walnut cake afterwards as a reward.

How did it go?

You can also try stroking a cat or a dog or a rabbit, something furry. A screaming hairy armadillo won't work because they actually scream if you touch them, which is not exactly conducive to what we're trying to achieve here, but with the others it soothes them as well as us, which is a bonus. It releases all kinds of lovely hormones to make you feel better and lowers your blood pressure. A furry cushion can work too if you don't have immediate access to a live creature that won't scream at you.

I find certain smells really soothing. I love an incense stick (much to my husband's annoyance), and find frank-incense and myrrh particularly comforting. I've had a long think about why this is and I've concluded it's probably because I'm Jesus, which is a turn-up for the books, isn't it?

I also like the smell of coffee, clothes that have dried outside, burning wood and petrol. I'm not sure how much petrol Jesus got to smell, so my theory of being the risen Christ might have a few flaws in it.

Fire does something hypnotic to me. I love the scent but find the flames intoxicating and they send me off into a beautifully altered state. The sea does this too. I can watch wave after wave after wave after wave after wave after wave after wave after wave — sorry, nodded off there — come and go for hours. As my friend Glenn says,

'When things are shit, head to the sea.' Now Glenn is no poet, as you can tell, but he's absolutely right.

The beauty of fire and the sea is their unpredictability and heritage. They are elements that we've lived with and needed to survive for centuries; that taps into something very primitive in all of us and helps our stress.

Make sure your home is a soothing place to be too. You may not be able to afford an Olympic-sized infinity pool or a six-foot fire pit, so we have to look at ways to make our nest as restful as possible.

If you can, find a specific place where you relax. It could be a room in your house where you have houseplants and the sun comes in in the afternoon. Could be a corner of the living room where you have a chair by your bookcase.

Or you could put a much-loved blanket on your bed when you need time to destress. Or maybe head to the shed in your garden with a cup of tea and a packet of biscuits to dunk. The environment matters, but so does using the space for rest on a regular basis so that you associate it with relaxation.

Use whatever sounds and music work for you too. Recordings of birdsong. Rainforest noises. I particularly like listening to thunder and lightning for some reason – I think it's the feeling of being safe when outside there's chaos.

Experiment with what works. Write down the techniques that work the best and keep the note as a reminder.

26. Get some Eaziwins!

I'm having a conversation with my husband after dinner one evening. He's on his phone concentrating very hard.

> ME: What on earth are you doing? You look like the cat trying to work out if he can catch that massive seagull.

> HIM: I'm playing this really hard word game.

> ME: I thought you had a stressful day, why are you playing a difficult word game?

> HIM: Bugger. Damn, that should be 'squirrel'. Why isn't it squirrel? It's got two 'r's for goodness sake.

> ME: Yeah, I really can't answer that question for you, strange man.

> HIM: What?

> ME: You were talking about squirrels.

> HIM: Yes! It's horrible.

> ME: Then why are you doing it?

HIM: No, the word. The word is 'horrible'.

ME: Again, why are you playing this game?

HIM: Because it gives me an eaziwin!

ME: Eaziwin? Sounds like a new gambling app.

HIM: Well, it's not.

ME: And gawd, I bet you're spelling that with a 'z' aren't you?

HIM: I am.

ME: And an unnecessary exclamation mark at the end?

HIM: Oh yes!

ME: Thought so.

HIM: I do eaziwins! when I'm stressed. I do something relatively simple that I can achieve so that I feel better about myself.

ME: You do know your self-esteem isn't based on whether you can spell the word 'horrible', don't you?

HIM: Of course I do, you moron. These kind of games give me a small rush of adrenalin and a shot of dopamine that help me process my stress. When I feel I'm failing at life, at least I can get an eaziwin! And spell 'horrible'.

ME: Better than smelling horrible, I guess.

Lots of things can give you an eaziwin! No, sorry, stop, stop. I'm going to have to drop the exclamation mark, the 'z' is bad enough.

Whether it's sudoku or crosswords, any brain puzzles are great, but so is clearing out the cupboard you've been meaning to sort out. Or finally getting round to retouching that bit of paint on the skirting board that got chipped, or trying a new recipe – anything small, achievable and relatively quick. If the recipe involves seventeen ingredients including plucking saffron from individual crocuses and then marinading in Provençal garlic for twenty-five days, I'd give it a miss.

Other eaziwins I do include dusting, planting bulbs, brushing the cat, plumping cushions, getting the duvet to the bottom of the cover so you don't have that flopping bit at the top when you're sleeping, and naming capital cities of countries. Niche, yes, but it doesn't matter as long as you do it well and quickly.

Stress impacts on our self-esteem to a really massive degree. Our confidence takes a huge battering. We feel like a failure for not managing. Which is why eaziwins are brilliant.

When we're living with and tackling stress on a day-to-day basis, it really pays to get these eaziwins under your belt. On the surface they might seem pointless but trust me, they're not – they're evidence that you can achieve stuff.

Give a bit of thought to what your eaziwins could be and then give it a try to see if you get the little rush of accomplishment.

I tried to do sudoku on the train once and got so cross I threw my phone on the table and cracked the screen, which didn't help my stress. It's got to be a little bit taxing to make you feel like you've achieved something, but not so difficult that it makes you more stressed.

You can also keep a record of your eaziwins. It's amazing how they build up after a few days to give you evidence of your achievements.

Also, please note I have trademarked Eaziwin! Any gambling apps can contact me directly please.

27. Become an Olympic hurdler

You're at the starting blocks of the one-hundred-metre hurdles at the Olympic Games.

You've got a new skin-tight lycra suit on. You give dagger-like stares to the other competitors, and you've invented a cool hand symbol for when the camera pans to you. You do a few warm-up jumps and then get on the starting line.

The gun goes off. You see all the hurdles in front of you and the finishing line at the end. You blast off the blocks and think, 'I'm a *really, really* good hurdler. I've been training for years. I don't need to jump them one at a time, I can get over them all in one massive jump. Easy.'

I'll let you fill in the mental image of what happens next.

It might seem clichéd and simplistic to say, 'Take one step at a time' but when you're in the middle of the chaos and uncertainty of stress, it's easy to forget.

Our now injured hurdler did a great job at visualising

where he wanted to be, but not such a good job at doing the steps to get there.

You have to do both. Visualise and plan. In steps.

Just like the hurdles, you have to narrow the gap of where you want to get to slowly, in order to make things easier. If we just fixate on the final outcome, it will seem massive, and you'll possibly fall because it feels too huge, and you haven't looked at the steps to get there.

So, if your goal is to make your life less hectic, you need a clear image of what it will look like. Then look at the hurdles that you will need to clear to achieve this. Get your parents in to look after the kids one day. Use afterschool clubs. Use gin and tonics.

If you want to reduce your workload, you have to take the steps to get there. Talk to your boss. Don't take on extra work. Say no to things. Be strict with your time management. Delegate.

If you want to eat a pineapple, you don't shove the whole thing in your mouth. That would be silly and spiky. You take one chunk at a time; then you don't end up in hospital, which is always good.

I once was being bullied at work. It was horrendous and ridiculous, and my stress was colossal.

I had to manage my daily tasks as well as this stupid guy making remarks about my competency every few hours. 'I see you haven't got that report done yet, James,'

111

he would say. Or 'I just want to say, James, I really disagreed with what you said in that meeting.' He was, if you'll excuse my language, a complete and utter scullion dick splash.

He also had the desk behind me, so it was hard to ignore him. But during the times he was gone, I started to make plans.

Hiring a trained assassin to take him out in the canteen wasn't an option unfortunately (assassins are seriously expensive), so I had to look at other ways to get what I wanted – namely for him to stop bullying me. This wasn't going to happen instantly, so I had to consider the hurdles and jump them one at a time.

The first step was to ignore his remarks. Not respond, not defend myself, not get angry. No reaction at all.

Second step was to write down what he said, and the date and time he said it.

Third step was to talk to my boss and tell them what was happening.

Fourth step was to get support from my friends and family.

Fifth step was to go to a meeting with me, my boss and the scullion dick splash. He was challenged on his remarks and apologised, explaining that he was under stress because his wife had left him after his numerous affairs, and he was taking it out on me. Between you and me, I think she made a fantastic decision, but you're not allowed to say that in these type of meetings.

Sixth step was for me to reluctantly accept his apology (through really, really, really gritted teeth).

Seventh step was to enjoy not being bullied, and get back to work. And still secretly hate him.

I couldn't have got to the seventh step without carefully thinking about and implementing the previous steps – it just wouldn't have worked.

Remember, your stress *will* get easier if you take it one step, one hurdle or one pineapple chunk at a time.

113

28. Just badger off

It's time to get really angry.

Don't worry, I'm not going to send you to the head teacher's office for a right royal telling off – we're going to get cross with stress instead. That sounds better, doesn't it?

Anger is a great motivational tool for stress because it gives you power back and you don't feel at the mercy of all the things happening to you.

Now, anger can't necessarily get rid of the causes of your stress. If you're made redundant, getting cross isn't going to give you your job back but hey, you can get furious with the numbskull CEO who made the decision – feel free to create a voodoo doll. They probably don't work, but it's worth a try, eh?

What we get angry at is the *impact* the stress is having on us. We get cross at the way that it's ruling our lives – consuming all our time and energy. To do that, we turn stress into an external thing, something imaginary to focus our frustrations on.

My stress is a dodgy badger.

I honestly have no idea why, it's just what seems to work. I've nothing intrinsically against badgers you understand. I loved the only badger I've ever seen, but this badger wears dark glasses, constantly smokes stinky cigars, wears a trilby hat, is running one of those pyramid selling schemes and has a bunch of knock off watches on the inside of his raincoat. He's a manipulative pillock of a badger. He's determined to get me involved in shady dealings and make my life a complete misery.

When I think of my stress, I imagine this badger trying to take over my life and ruin me, financially, emotionally and physically, and then I get really flipping angry.

115

I don't want stress to rule my life and spoil everything. I want to enjoy my job (contrary to popular belief, we are supposed to). I want to be able to switch off at the end of the day. I want to go on holiday and not think about all the emails and work undone. I want my free time to be as relaxing as possible, not spent dreading every message that comes through on my phone in case it's an old flame wanting to be abusive or some troll on social media telling me what an idiot I am. I don't want to be up at three o'clock in the morning fretting about things I can't control or haven't achieved.

I WILL NOT BE RULED BY THE BLOODY BADGER!

I want you to think about what your stress would look like. Maybe call it by a ridiculous name, maybe make it an animal, maybe make it a monster. Don't make it too cute though, because it's hard to get cross with a cuddly panda named Blossom, and don't give it a name you associate with anyone you know and like.

You can create some characteristics like I did with my badger. Things that you really hate. Maybe you loathe liars, cheaters, self-centredness, big egos, greed, vanity, arrogance; whatever gets you fuming, you should use. You might want to take all the characteristics from your ex for example – that might work, eh?

The next thing that we do is talk back to our badger.

We get really cross about the impact stress is having on our life. You can swear. You can raise your voice. You can punch them, anything to reduce its power and give **you** the power back to take action and move forward.

I use a loud kind of 1960s East London shouty gangster voice. 'Oi, you! You over there. Mr so-called stress badger. You ain't taking me down, you think you will but you ain't got the power guv'nor. I'm going to sort this because I am better than you. I am going to get on with my life. I ain't going under. Now do one, you massive dodgy black and white smelly pillock.'

See how it gets you riled up? Good, isn't it? Please don't go and hit any actual badgers by the way.

Try having a go at yours – see how it feels to turn your stress into a thing and then let loose.

29. Humour me, okay?

What do you call a fish with no eyes?
A fsh.

I know. I know. I'm sorry.

But tell me, did you grin a little? Did you groan with mock disdain? Chuckle a bit? Did you get some momentary relief from your stress? Or maybe you're still on the floor holding your stomach, tears streaming down your face going, 'James, I tell ya, no one tells them like you do, NO ONE. Dear me I've never laughed so much, oops, I think my spleen just came out.'

I have plenty more jokes of this quality by the way, just send me an email.

When I'm stressed, I deliberately watch funny television, YouTube clips or podcasts. Often, I go back to comedy that I know will make me laugh again because the thing about comedy is that it lifts you. It raises you up and your stress goes down. It lets you see the lightness in the world, the absurdity and the glee. It makes you see that there is laughter and fun and the world is not always a terrible place.

I also use dark humour a lot, because again it lifts stress and makes it weird and surreal and I can get some perspective on things. A conversation with my sister:

> SISTER: How are you, James?
>
> ME: I'm so stressed.
>
> SISTER: How stressed out of one hundred?
>
> ME: Sixty-seven million.
>
> SISTER: That's not out of one hundred.
>
> ME: I failed maths GCSE three times, what do you expect?
>
> SISTER: For you to know the numbers one to one hundred.
>
> ME: Well, I'm so stressed I can't remember them.
>
> SISTER: Have you tried counting from one hundred backwards? I hear that's really good for stress.
>
> ME: Ha, bloody ha.

We then went on to talk about how I could manage my stress better, but it was good to change my mood, to not feel so weighed down by the seriousness of it all.

I'm not usually a fan of slapstick, but for some reason seeing comedians (in particular, Buster Keaton) fall over and do stunts really helps me when I'm stressed. Also, videos of people slipping on ice, tripping into a paddling pool, tumbling into some cow poo in a field, are all superbly beneficial. I don't want to see anyone genuinely hurt and there may be some worrying subconscious delight in seeing others in compromising positions, but let's not look too closely at that shall we.

Have you ever been having a really stressful conversation with friends? One where people are talking about their worries and burdens, and then suddenly someone does a massive burp and everyone laughs? It breaks the tension. Everyone groans and things seem less fraught.

Similarly, my family and I were gathered for my grandmother's funeral a few years ago. Everyone was upset, worried about how the day would go. Then I spilt a huge mug of coffee (with a decent dollop of whisky in it) onto my mother's cream carpet. Not intentionally of course. It had us all crying with laughter. Thankfully the carpet was being replaced the following week or my mum may not have found it quite so amusing.

A colleague of mine had a great technique with her children when they were all screaming, crying and having tantrums – she fell to the floor and kicked her legs in the air and said 'wibble, wibble'. They had no idea what was going on, but it made them giggle and forget what they were stressed about. Now, she had to keep changing what she did each time to keep it original, which caused *her* some stress, but you get my point here.

Or think about the importance of Christmas cracker jokes. Seriously, they're vital. Everyone is gathered around the table for lunch, you've mistakenly invited the neighbour who starts to make lewd comments about the importance of men basting the turkey; your father-in-law is sighing at the state of the sprouts because he likes them on a light boil at the start of November; the kids have already eaten seventeen chocolate bars for breakfast and are dancing on their chairs; and your partner has fallen asleep after drinking mulled wine for breakfast. You suggest pulling the crackers and read out the first joke. It's so cheesy you could have it on a cracker with some pickle. Then everyone takes turns to put their hat on and read their own joke. It breaks the tension; it brings everyone together. You all look ridiculous. You all tell appalling jokes and things are just that bit better.

There's a reason why comedy and entertainment are so loved and timeless. We need a break. We need to be taken out of our current state for a while and to see the other side of life – the lighter, happier, funnier side that stress shields us from. Stress is like an eclipse and you can't see the bloody sun.

You may not feel that you want to watch anything funny when you're stressed because it all feels like too much and you don't think you'll laugh at all. But that's exactly why you should.

Two windmills are standing on a wind farm.
One asks, 'What's your favourite type of music?'
The other says, 'I'm a big metal fan.'

Oh, come on now, that was a good one.

30. Just get rid of stuff

Let's get shredding, and I'm not talking about lettuce here.   123

When stress is punching me in the soft ouchy parts, I get busy and get rid of stuff. It's sort of like a ritual I have. It helps massively.

Generally, we all have too much stuff – apart from books, you can never have too many books. But other things we amass, sometimes without thinking and other times because we've convinced ourselves we'll definitely need a decades-old rusty nail and put in in the desk drawer in case of emergencies.

When it's all getting on top of me, I sit down, sort and shred.

You can find me in the kitchen by the cabinet going through Tupperware I thought would be useful for a picnic but hasn't been used in twenty years. Sorting out sixteen different types of spoons for draining pasta. Mumbling about the ludicrousy of having silver plated fish knives when I just use normal knives. So, it all gets chucked out.

Some to recycling. Some to charity. Some reluctantly in the bin if it can't be reused. It feels damn good.

Then I'll head into the sitting room and into the dark, dark subterranean depths of the bottom desk drawer where earthlings have ne'er dwelt for fifty thousand years. I'll look through old bank statements, TV licence receipts, hospital appointment letters, excessive amounts of bubble wrap and envelopes which I thought would be useful but are so old the glue has solidified and the paper browned to Egyptian parchment. Shred, shred, recycle. Bam.

Then on to the wardrobe and I sort through clothes that a moth has been silently snacking on for months. Trousers that have holes in obscene places but I've hung onto them because I think at some point I'll take up sewing and patch them up with a jaunty overlock stitch. Jumpers that I can't even remember buying. Shirts that I look at and think 'You looked like a plonker wearing that when you were eighteen, do you really think that it's going to suddenly look good on you now?' A jacket I can't even get my arms into for some reason, and numerous coats that have been given to me or I've bought from Oxfam because they will be 'useful for winter' and then continue to wear the same duffel coat each year. Out it all goes. Recycle, recycle, charity shop. Bosh.

As I'm sorting, I go into a kind of semi-hypnotic state – at least it feels like that, it's when you're concentrating keenly on a task and everything else fades into the background. If you've ever seen a ten-year-old concentrating on a computer game, it's kind of like that.

The sorting itself is a break from the stress, and then whilst I recycle or give to charity or bin things, I think about my stress being held in those objects and *whoop* away it goes. Sounds odd I know, but give it a try. *Whoop*, the stuff goes into the recycling bin. *Wee* the piles of paper are fed through the teeth of the hungry shredder.

It feels like something has lifted. That things are a bit lighter. There's less stuff hanging over you and there's a sense that you can carry on managing your stress but in a better place.

125

I find organising also has the same impact. I finally sorted the drawer in my kitchen which held batteries, phone chargers, blu tack, paper clips, travel plug adapters, bin bags, tin foil and manuals for electric appliances I no longer have. Why am I keeping the instructions on how to defrost the freezer for a freezer I don't own anymore?

I bought two big colourful cardboard boxes from the internet (without measuring them properly but fortunately they fitted well). I divided everything into electrical and non-electrical. Not exactly the height of organisational sophistication, but nevertheless it really helped my stress. I look at the boxes and it just makes me feel better that I can get things done.

As bizarre as it sounds, I also leave things aside to organise for when my stress is high. Currently, I have a blue box file full of paper that needs sorting out. There's nothing urgent I need to look at, so it's waiting for when my stress is high again and I can reorganise it. When it's time, it will feel good, and it will do my stress good.

31. Turn everything off, for a little bit

127

We've all read those articles online. You know the ones titled 'Turn off Tuesday' when you're supposed to not use your phone, not log on to social media or look at the news and just sit in a wheat field pretending to be a pale-throated sloth.

This is all very well but it's just not as easy as that when you rely on maps to get you to the wheat field, you have to pay for the parking on your phone, you have to find out how hot it's going to be on the weather app and, of course, you want to take a selfie pretending to be a sloth.

I gave 'Turn off Tuesday' a go once. I left my phone at home and headed to work. It was a Wednesday actually, but I didn't think the Tuesday was prescriptive. It was all fairly hellish.

I realised that: a) I had booked an e-ticket for my train journey to work which was on my phone and so I had to pay for another paper ticket; b) I didn't get a sense of connection with myself, I just felt a lack of connection with my loved ones; and c) I saw a cat whose black fur formed a twirly moustache and I couldn't take a photo. When I got home, I wanted to lick my phone I was so happy, and that's just not something you want to see a middle-aged man doing.

I tried again after I realised I went cold turkey too fast. This time I went to the beach, which is at the end of my road, and didn't take my phone. Now, you might be thinking, 'That's a bit crap, James', and you'd be absolutely right, but I went for half an hour and it was a start eh?

For the first five minutes I kept thinking how nice it would be to do a selfie pretending to be seagull or film some waves. But then *not* having my phone made me focus on the waves more. I was just there in the moment. Staring.

After another fifteen minutes I felt a sort of sense of freedom. I couldn't check my phone every two minutes, so I just had to look at the sea. And the clouds doing their cloudy thing and children laughing and the sun dancing over the water and making it sparkle like a gaudy bracelet on a shopping channel. And it was really nice.

Yes, I felt a bit naked, a bit like part of me was missing, but in the end, I realised that wasn't a good feeling to have, and really that's why I was doing this – to try and disconnect from the virtual world and feel more attached to the actual world. To not jump at every text message, social media notification or email.

I got home and there had been no emergencies, no one had phoned me. I hadn't been offered a free round-the-world holiday via private jet, staying in five-star hotels and on yachts, just for being a jolly nice person. Barack Obama hadn't followed me on Twitter. I was a bit put out about that in particular, but I'm built of stronger stuff.

I built up these phone-less trips gradually, adding ten minutes at a time. Yes, it felt odd; yes, I worried about not being able to check the immediate weather conditions in Ho Chi Minh City, but slowly the good stuff outweighed the weird feeling.

Now, I go for walks without my phone regularly, which helps regulate my overall stress levels, but I purposely do this when my stress is really high. It helps me stay present, rather than worrying about 'what ifs' and thinking about the worse that can happen – neither of these thoughts get us anywhere by the way.

It means I see wonderful things that I wouldn't nor-mally. A couple asleep in their deckchairs holding hands; a dog taking secret licks of their owner's ice-cream; a yacht slipping silently across the horizon; a beautiful, speckled stone that uncovers itself and seems to say, 'This is for you James.'

I also limit my intake of world events I have no control

over. I've taken the news app off my phone so I'm not checking it every two minutes and I removed my social media apps; instead, I log in through Google which takes much longer, so I just do it once or twice a day.

Remember, the key is to do it for a bit. You don't have to go full hermit on me; just try it slowly and build up to maybe an hour or two.

And hey, Barack, follow me, I'm an absolute hoot.

32. Do something you're darn good at

When I'm stressed, I weed the garden.

Not just because it needs doing, which it always does, but because I'm bloody good at it.

I realise blowing your own trumpet is not the done thing, but sod it, I'm saying it loud, and I'm saying it proud, I'M GOOD AT WEEDING.

I can identify the weeds, make sure that I'm not picking my expensive dahlias by mistake and then pluck those blighters out of the ground, shake their roots free of soil and fling them into eternity (well the compost bin), never to be seen again. Hooray! I may start an annual pride march for expert weeders. 'We're here, we weed – let's grow together!' Okay, that's doesn't entirely work. Give me a few weeks, I'll get a better chant I promise.

Stress pushes us down. It makes us feel useless. Redundant. We think we're not good at anything and that thought will fester and grow if you let it. 'I can't manage my job.' 'I can't manage the kids.' 'I can't manage my relationship.' I can't, I can't, I can't. So we counteract it with doing stuff you **can** do.

My friend William crochets. When he's really stressed, he gets the hooks out and makes amazing scarves, because he's good at it. No matter how modest he is about them, they look really great. He did a crochet course, called 'No way! It's Amazing Crochet with the lovely Faye!' ... Okay, it wasn't called that, but that's what every crochet course should be called in my opinion.

He learned to be a great scarf maker so when stress hits, he relies on the skills he's built up. He knows he can do a brilliant half double stitch and away he goes, proving that stress is wrong.

My cousin Charlotte can strip down a vintage Austin

A40 car. She's spent the last three years putting it back together. She knows how to attach the chassis to the wheel arches and then put the engine into the ... well, I've no idea what, but she's doing it and it's pretty impressive. When she's stressed, she goes into her garage and fiddles and welds and connects things because she knows how to do it and it makes her feel better. She's now on one of those car forums and shows people what she's done and gives people advice.

133

In case you were wondering (and I knew you were), this is not the same as the Eaziwins! of Chapter 26, which are about quick satisfaction. This is about your skills, your talents, things that you've learnt to do over the years and can rely on to make you feel better about yourself.

You might be an excellent cook; perhaps you've taken years to master the ultimate curry, getting the perfect combination of seeds and herbs balancing with the vegetables. Or maybe you've finally got that sourdough starter to create a perfect loaf after months of it flopping in the oven like a wet fish. Perhaps you've conquered a sublime croque-en-bouche and it's now taller than your Aunty Sheila, and she's six-foot-two out of her heels.

My husband is a superb cocktail maker. He's completely perfected making a Mary Pickford – a prohibition drink, named after the actress. After a long time of my eyes exploding and me spluttering, 'Jeez, how much cherry liqueur did you put in this, you maniac?' he's got the measures completely balanced and it's delicious.

Take a pause, get out your phone or a piece of paper and write down some of the things you can do well, because you've learnt how to do them. This can include skills that you do in your job, but if your work is causing you stress it's not a good idea to include those. Try and think about things you have learnt as life has unfolded. Flower arranging, building a computer, playing cricket, a video game you're good at, pruning the roses for spring.

We need gratification and a self-esteem boost when stress is on our shoulders so we can stand a bit straighter, hold our stress with more balance and control.

33. Mini-me moments

I want you to take three months off because you flipping   135
well deserve it.

You're going to a remote island in the South Pacific that
is accessible only at sunset. There's a staff of sixty to cater
to your every need. You get pedicures and manicures by
clicking your fingers, the chef has implanted a microchip
inside your stomach and at the slightest whiff of hunger he
appears by your side with food you've never heard of but
instantly adore. A bath, liberally sprinkled with organic
rose petals imported from the foothills of the Cotopaxi
volcano in Ecuador, is run for you every half an hour just
in case you need it. Labrador puppies come and cuddle
you on demand, but these can be exchanged for fluffy
white kittens if you so desire. The sea is kept at a constant
temperature of thirty-five degrees and the exact turquoise
colour is closely monitored to ensure it's consistent across
your field of vision.

Let's be clear, this is not what I mean by ensuring you

get some me time, although it would be nice, wouldn't it?

When you have four kids, a full-time job, a Spanish giant rabbit with a dodgy stomach, a car that has failed its MOT, and you forgot to do the supermarket delivery order so have to make dinner from two eggs, some cornflakes and a tin of baked beans, it's not easy to get some time for yourself.

A few years ago, I had a job which meant most days I was running from one end of the city to the other delivering training. I was getting constant texts from the people renovating my bathroom with questions including, 'Do you think an antique gold bidet would complement the baroque taps?' and, 'Have you thought about a triple Amazonian shower head?' I would then head home to neighbours who thought that playing 1990s neurofunk drum and bass was acceptable at three o'clock in the morning, and then got upset when I knocked on their door in my pyjamas looking somewhat displeased.

I searched Google and found one of those 'Relax your mind in one easy step' clickbait articles.

'You need to get some time to yourself. Pamper YOU. Indulge in the gloriousness that is YOU. With this new seaweed and tomato ketchup soap you will never be stressed again, EVER, EVER, EVER. Totally real customer Jeanette from Tewkesbury says, "Like, OMG, I'm

like just so relaxed now and everything, it's just super
amazing and everything." Order one standard size bar in
*three easy payments of £350. *Terms and conditions apply;*
you might not feel relaxed at all and sometimes
the soap leaves poisonous and permanent lesions on
your skin.'

I closed the tab and phoned my friend Geoff.

ME: I have no idea what to do, I'm not getting any time
to myself at all. I just run around all day getting more
and more stressed.

GEOFF: Hmmm . . . I hear you, have you tried mini-me
moments?

ME: I'm sorry?

GEOFF: Mini-me moments.

ME: Have you quit your job at the pub and now you're
working for an advertising agency flogging chocolate
and caramel-based snacks?

GEOFF: I have quit my job at the pub actually, but
you've been too busy to ask. Listen, sometimes it's
impossible to get enough time to relax so you have to
take small moments for yourself, or as I call them—

ME: Mini-me moments – yes, I get it.

GEOFF: It's like when we were busy at the pub and it
was just one irritating customer after another—

ME: But that's my local!

GEOFF: I know. What's your point?

ME: Fine, fine, carry on.

GEOFF: I had to find times when I could just breathe a little, so I take a few minutes in the loo, just focus on my breath, remind myself who I am—

ME: A bit of a rude friend?

GEOFF: . . . and then I carry on. I do the same at home when the kids are fighting over who has the biggest toenails or some such nonsense; I sit in the hall, usually the dog comes and sits with me, and we take a moment to regroup.

ME: Okay. Well, I'll try. Have you got a new job? It's not selling soap is it?

Geoff didn't get a job with the ridiculous soap people, he went to work in a different pub, with better clientele apparently, and a nicer toilet to have mini-me moments in.

I took Geoff's advice and take mini-me moments when I'm feeling stressed and need to collect myself and when I don't have enough time to jet off and cuddle Labrador puppies.

I take a deep breath, focus on me – I don't do anything special, usually I just go, 'My name is James, I like yoghurt and books and cats' and then take a deep breath. It takes seconds but it is enough to stop the stress spinning my world around.

It's a momentary pause, a time to re-group, a small but powerful moment to concentrate on you.

34. Exceptional ways of accepting stuff you don't want to accept

My friend is moving away and I'm not happy.

In fact, it's causing me huge stress. She's the person I can phone in the morning when I'm not feeling good. We can go for a coffee or naughty lunchtime cocktails, put the world to rights, give each other advice, a hug and space to feel crap without worrying we're burdening each other. It's one of those lovely reciprocal friendships that are rare and to be cherished.

Who am I going to talk to now? Who's going to say, 'Yes, let's try that cocktail with cranberry juice, brandy, whisky, gin, absinthe and vodka. But shall we leave the cranberry juice?' Who's going to listen to me whine about the price of yoghurt and the bins not being collected on time, without stifling a yawn?

But there's nothing I can do about it. She's moving to live nearer her mother who's getting older and needs more help.

It's slightly unfair for me to say, 'I know your mother needs you, that she gave birth to you, that she lives alone with no family or friends nearby . . . but when you think about it, I'm much, much more important than her, don't you think?'

I can't hold her captive in my shed and feed her flatbread through the gap in the door, and it's probably unfair to superglue myself to her, or take her on a plane to Fox Island in Alaska and feed her passport to a passing brown bear.

The more I rail against it, the worse it gets. The more I try and deny it's going to happen, the more stressed I feel. And it changes nothing. Finally, I consider having a full-blown toddler-esque tantrum and calling her a 'potty bum face', but my husband advises against it to save what's left of my already shattered dignity.

I have to accept it, as much as I don't want to. I feel sad but finally I acknowledge it's going to happen.

We make firm plans to meet every two months. I'll go and stay with her, she'll come and stay with me, and once a year we will book a hotel in London for the weekend and explore new cocktail bars, always asking the bar staff to 'leave the mixer' when we order a drink. I feel sad but pleased we've made plans, and, most importantly, less stressed because I've accepted it.

Acceptance is a key skill to managing life in general, and especially important when managing stress.

It doesn't mean laying down like a doormat. It doesn't mean inaction. It doesn't mean shrugging and going 'Meh, so what'. It means seeing your stress for what it is. It means not sticking your head in the sand. It means accepting what's going on. It's not convincing yourself it's all okay really.

A friend of mine was recently ill, life-threateningly ill. I wasn't sure he would make it. I didn't want him to be ill. I spent a lot of time cursing the gods, shaking my fist at the sky and trying to manage my stress about the situation and failing miserably. Maybe the doctors had made a mistake? Maybe he wasn't ill after all? Maybe the medical records had got mixed up somehow.

People said to me, 'I'm sure he'll be fine,' which didn't ultimately help and just colluded with my denial. What helped was to accept that he was seriously ill, not rally against reality.

Again, remember that accepting our stress is a great way of actually managing it. It's not trying to turn it three-hundred-and-sixty degrees and go, 'I am SO eternally pleased this is happening to me because it's going to be a superb learning experience on my personal journey to self-actualisation; my gratitude is overflowing' – sod that, stress is crap.

What I mean is accepting that stress is happening, not denying it, is really important to moving on with your life and being able to tackle it.

35. Bigger picture, like the ones you find in the Louvre

143

In this chapter we're going to time travel – exciting, eh? Who knew that was going to happen when you started reading this book? But first a conversation I had with my grandmother when she was one-hundred-and-four.

We're in her bungalow, she's made an apple crumble, which I'm currently demolishing with a large dollop of squirty cream. We're looking out onto the communal gardens in the retirement complex she lives in. I'm stressing about a job interview I've got coming up.

GRANDMOTHER: The thing is, when you get to my age you realise all the things that do matter, and the things that don't. You get the whole bigger picture.

ME: And iff gussing wurying abut smll stff dont mutter?

GRANDMOTHER: Finish eating before you speak, honestly.

ME: [*swallowing*] Sorry. And I'm guessing worrying about small stuff doesn't matter?

GRANDMOTHER: Exactly, don't sweat the small stuff – or, more importantly, realise what the small stuff is first and then don't sweat it.

ME: Isn't that the same thing?

GRANDMOTHER: No. Awareness first, then action.

ME: Right. So, how do you know what the small stuff is?

GRANDMOTHER: Well, in very general terms it's the annoying neighbour who puts the rubbish out on the wrong day . . .

ME: . . . do you mean Jean next door?

GRANDMOTHER: The person at church who never washes the teaspoons . . .

ME: . . . isn't Jean in charge of washing cutlery?

GRANDMOTHER: The woman who says she's going to rake up her leaves from the garden but never does . . .

ME: . . . gran, Jean is ninety-eight and that's a particularly leafy tree she's got.

GRANDMOTHER: All those things aren't worth the stress. Trust me. You have to look at the bigger picture.

ME: So, what is the bigger picture?

GRANDMOTHER: It's family and friends. Above all, it's knowing that love matters.

ME: Okay.

GRANDMOTHER: And always, always visit your grand-mother, brush your teeth, do as much travelling as you can whilst you're young, and when I die don't give her next door this apple crumble recipe.

ME: Isn't that an example of stressing about something small?

GRANDMOTHER: No, that's an example of stressing about something very, very important indeed.

ME: Fine, I promise.

GRANDMOTHER: Good boy. Now, don't hog the cream and don't worry about the job interview, you can only do your best.

I want you to fast forward to one-hundred-and-four as well; you don't need to be worried about your apple crumble recipe, I promise.

You're going to look back on your life and play it like a film in your head with all the good stuff that's happened or might happen, which could include going to school, jobs you've had, relationships, children, grandchildren, nieces, nephews, friendships, pets, holidays – anything significant, anything that made you smile.

Now, think about your stress – how important do you think it will be when you get to old age? Will you still be fretting about a job interview? A silly argument with a neighbour? Your boss telling you to work harder? I don't think so and that's the perspective we need to have today.

Essentially, I'm telling you to be more like my one-hundred-and-four-year-old grandmother. Her name was Joyce, but you don't need to change your name, just change your viewpoint a bit.

Since the conversation with my grandmother, I realised that it's never, ever worth being in a job that keeps you up at night, it's never worth being in a relationship that makes you miserable, it's never worth creating more conflict over small things, it's never worth worrying if people don't like you.

You have to pick your battles carefully. Now for Joyce, her battle with Jean next door seemed totally worth it, and to be fair I've never given her apple crumble recipe away to anyone. We have to think, 'is this worth my energy and time in the long run?'

We're much better saving ourselves for the big times when we need to manage big stress.

Most importantly, as Joyce would say, concentrate on love, concentrate on relationships, concentrate on experiences and people that are meaningful because at one-hundred-and-four (or whatever age we get to) we will have fewer regrets, and by living our lives now we have less stress.

36. Don't delay, no way, it's not okay to delay, go out of your way to not delay

I was once in a teaching job that was so ridiculously stressful, I would've been perfectly happy to have imploded instead, to have turned into stellar material and formed a new supernova in space.

I had no job induction, no course guide to follow, no initial support, no permanent contract. I was being paid about 50p every other month and suddenly there was a large group of sixteen-year-old students waiting for me to teach them. This was not good. As the weeks before my first lesson went by my stress levels rose higher than a group of giraffes forming an acrobatic pyramid.

The more I thought about my first lesson the more stressed I got; the more stressed I got the more I convinced myself I knew nothing and would start the lecture with the word 'grhhbbennenenjk' coming out of my mouth and then probably some dribbling. Definitely lots of dribbling.

So, I delayed preparing for it. Instead, I cleaned the flat. I planted some geraniums. I brushed a very uncooperative but now beautiful-looking cat. I cleaned out my wardrobe and decided this was absolutely the completely and utterly best time to put all of my books into alphabetical order – I have about eight hundred books, just to put you in the picture.

Eventually, the night before my first day at work came around. I did some work but felt woefully unprepared, funnily enough. Then in the morning because of the sheer amount of stress, I left my lecture notes at home and had to invent most of the Health and Social Care Act 2012. Tricky, to say the least.

> ME: Grhhbbennenenjk. I mean, err . . . good morning. Sorry, that's a bit of dribble there, just wipe that up. Yeah. So, like the umm . . . the Health and Social Care Act 2011.
>
> SMART ALEC: 2012.
>
> ME: Yeah, that's right! Just testing. Full marks for you. Just a little quiz to start with. The act, which came into fruition—
>
> SMART ALEC: Fruition?
>
> ME: Law? Yes law. Is like, well, it's, like, just totally concerned with being nice to other people and, like, caring for others and shit.

SMART ALEC: Did you just swear?

ME: I was talking in the vernacular about the personal hygiene of vulnerable people . . . which is sometimes . . . a task? Yes, a task, when you work in health and social care. And some of those tasks are covered in the Health and Social Care Act of 2011.

SMART ALEC: 2012.

ME: WHAT DO YOU WANT FROM ME?!

This was painful. Actually painful. Needless to say, the rest of the lecture did not go well. Eventually, on a whim, I decided the remainder of the hour should be spent with the students discussing with each other what *they* thought was in the Health and Social Care Act of 2012, writing it down on the smart board and then next week I would check and make sure they knew it. Dear me.

Two things I learnt from that day. One, don't take a job without an induction or support and, secondly, delaying tackling your stress only makes it worse. It never, ever helps. Trust me.

Of course, the temptation with stress is to avoid it, to delay dealing with it, because it's painful and traumatic. Our natural response is to not want to feel, experience, examine or manage what's causing us pain.

We spend a lot of our lives avoiding or masking our

pain. Sometimes, that's fine. If you've broken your leg, some painkillers are definitely going to be needed.
But with stress it's a little different. We have to look at what's causing it, we have to examine and deal with it, or everything gets worse and worse and worse.

Once we develop a pattern of examining our stress and managing it head on, and at the time, it becomes easier to cope with.

When you find yourself holding your hands over your ears, closing your eyes and going 'No, no, no. Bugger off!' in reaction to your stress — that, my friend, is delaying.

It's fine to catch yourself doing it. Don't give yourself a hard time about it. Hey, I catch myself doing that all the time. The trick is to then do something about the delaying.

37. Mix it up (and your cocktails)

Now, if you've read Chapter 16 you might be going, 'Whoa there mister, hold your horses one second now, you were talking about the importance of hanging on to structure and stable things, and now you're talking about mixing it up. What is *with* you?'

Well, yes, but the thing is different stress strategies work at different times, so sometimes routine is absolutely crucial and other times changing things in your life really helps to get a different perspective on your stress. I'm not just being deliberately contrary, you'll be pleased to know.

Stress seems endless. You're a hamster on a wheel but some fool has blocked the exit, so you just keep going round and round trying to get out and getting more and more exhausted.

My friend Sam (not a hamster) got stuck in this way. Their job was dull and repetitive — which is stressful in itself, not all of our stress comes from extremes. They were caring for their great aunt, who was in a residential home but needed lots of jobs done and a complicated will sorting out.

All the dates they went on were with people who declared that they 'never dated people who rent flats', and one admitted that he only really liked people with oblong faces. Another near miss was a guy who made paper puppets of his exes. I saw a photo of these puppets and they would scare the bejesus out of Beelzebub himself. Lastly, their flatmate was an asshole who thought washing up was for losers. What is with some people?

A break was needed. A shake-up was needed. A cocktail was needed.

Sam moved into a new flat with much nicer people who understood the concept of clean crockery and the joy of a mojito. It was closer to their work, so they got home earlier and went to evening classes, which broke up the monotony of work. No, Sam didn't find the love of their life in a 'build a puppet of your ex-lover' class, but they did stop dating for a while which reduced the stress considerably and had the added bonus of them not forking out money for average tasting meals with idiots.

At times you need to make big changes that can seem really scary, but will pay dividends in the long run. I've often changed jobs because the stress just wasn't worth it. I went for a relatively well-paid job, enough for a couple of holidays and a bottle of gin every so often, to a much lower paid job *but* it was significantly less stressful. And it was totally and utterly worth it. It really was. I couldn't take lavish holidays to the Seychelles for three months (okay, I couldn't do that before), but my everyday life was so much calmer. I slept, I didn't worry as much, it was all so much easier.

Even small changes can help stress. I get off that hamster wheel and try new things. I might take a different route to work, change my night-time routine, buy some different food, read a book that I wouldn't normally choose, buy some silly socks. The sock thing can work wonders by the way, but they have to be really ridiculous. I favour colourful stripes but polka dots, cartoon characters or offensive slogans can all work.

When you change things in your life, sometimes the stress goes. Sometimes it just feels easier to manage because other things become enjoyable. Sometimes it gives you a different perspective on what's going on.

When I mix things up it's like shaking a snow globe, things fall differently than they did before.

When you shake up your world you shake the stress.

153

38. So tell me, what's worked before?

I get support for my mental health, because it's up and down like a hyperactive, sugar-fuelled yo-yo.

Some of it I can manage by myself. Other times, when things aren't so good, I need support from others. Very often when I'm contacting a support service, the person on the other end will ask me, 'What's worked when you felt stress like this before James?'

In all honesty, most of the times I want to reply, 'Well, thank you for asking, Sarah. I've found hard drugs really help; particularly heroin, although I'm a bit of a crack cocaine fan too in fact – anything class A hits the spot. Sometimes – and you're going to love this, Sarah – sometimes, I'll just down a whole litre bottle of single malt whisky. Have you tried an Aberdour? Other times I'll do a bungee jump in Altopiano di Asiago, the Province of *Vicenza*, Italy, I'm sure you know the place. They do a lovely cheese nearby in Asiago; it's quite crumbly, good in a panini. I also find skydiving particularly helpful. I don't know about you, Sarah, but I like a thirty-thousand-foot drop. Just to add that sense of foreboding death to the proceedings. It's weird, it just all really, really helps me.'

I hate being asked this question but, as much as I hate to admit it, it's an important question to ask ourselves when we're stressed.

Stress has this weird way of making us forget that we've got through other times of stress, and what we did to manage it at the time.

I sit down and think, how did I manage when I was going through that relationship break up? Or when I had only £3 in my bank account? Or when I started that new job, or moved house, or was managing family issues? What did I do? How did I get through?

I think and then remember that I went for that walk, or talked to a particular friend, or changed my surroundings. I recall all the stuff that I had available to me and then consider if I can use those things now.

I want you to think about those times of stress in your own past. Try and examine those times in detail, uncomfortable as it might be, because it will give you great insight. Remember this will take a bit of head pain, and you might be there thinking, 'I've no idea what I did.' Or, 'I just carried on, but I've no idea how.' But look deeper, look

155

at specific times when it was really bad. Who was around you? What action did you take?

It can really pay to write it down somewhere, jot down all your thoughts around the time. Here's one of my times of stress, where I initially couldn't recall what I did but then it started to come as I wrote.

My friend dying:

* I found a bereavement forum online
* I talked to Lee's mum who knew my friend too
* I read some poetry about grief
* I read some books about grief
* I got support from other friends

Impossible as it may seem, you may even find some ways of managing that aren't in this book. I know, like, totally incredible.

39. Foresee the cyst

Okay, so forgive this slightly gross analogy but I have this tiny, weeny little cyst on my finger, it's barely noticeable.

If you looked at my fingers you'd go, 'Ooh, what lovely fingers you have, James, are you by any chance a professional hand model?' I'm not, by the way, in case you were wondering; I sucked my thumb as a child which made it slightly smaller than the other and I understand symmetry is key in the ruthless, competitive world of hand modelling.

Every time the cyst comes up and goes away again, I hope that it's gone for ever, and then I feel a bit crushed when it comes back. So, these days, rather than hoping its gone and being disappointed, I anticipate it coming. I don't like it when it comes back but I'm more prepared and it makes me less stressed.

I apply this principle to life which ultimately really helps my stress levels.

If I have a colleague I really like working with, rather

than thinking, 'I hope they never leave,' I think, 'They might leave at some point, they might get another job or get a promotion or retire.' I'll enjoy working with them day to day but also know there will be a day when I won't be working with them. When that comes, I'm sad but not as stressed as I would have been.

When my health is doing well, when I have no aches and pains, no mysterious cysts appearing on my finger destroying my modelling career, I'm grateful but I don't think that it's going to stay that way for ever because I know we all get ill at some stage. When I come down with flu or a stomach bug, I don't rally against it too much. Sure, I'm cross, I don't want it to happen, but I stockpile my favourite yoghurt and think, 'We all get ill, that's what happens.'

Knowing that stress in some form is around the corner means you can anticipate it and prepare for it. Please don't live your life looking for it, but just know it will come. This isn't a case of 'expect the worst', it's more a case of:

'Expect stress, know it's imminent and then it won't hit you in the face like an overzealous Bavarian dancer at a *Schuhplattler slap dance festival*.'

Admittedly, this is not as catchy, but it's more accurate.

Actually, I may make this into a motivational poster and sell it online, or etch it into bleached driftwood and hang it in the kitchen.

I don't want you to be on alert all the time, thinking, 'I could trip over that step,' or 'Oh my goodness that dog is going to poo on my car, I just know it.' That's not what I'm saying here. That type of hypervigilance is more a cause of stress rather than a way to manage it. It's just knowing that stress will come. That everything changes for the good and bad.

159

That Scouts have it right when they say, 'Be prepared'. Now, I left the Scouts after the second week when they wouldn't accommodate my requests for an organic Mediterranean vegetarian pizza with sourdough crust one evening. They weren't exactly prepared then, were they? But apart from that truly traumatising, life-altering incident, they've got a point.

I want to stay in my volunteer post because I enjoy it, but I also know that there will be stressful times. I might get a new supervisor I don't like. I might not be able to continue doing it physically. I might find that all of the other volunteers turn into murderous supernatural beings and things get a bit awkward in the staff room. You see, I've thought of everything, zombie apocalypse included.

I do this with death too. (Just lightening things up here.) I can rally against people and pets dying as much as I want but it won't stop it happening. Instead, I gently think about them dying. What I'll do to manage without them. What it will feel like. I picture myself in the future, crying, feeling lost, feeling sick, feeling empty. That image will help when it actually happens. Our imaginations are powerful tools.

By the way, this is not a case of me going, 'Just expect the worse. The world is doomed, DOOMED I tell you. Misery and slaughter will end our days. Prepare for calamity and the final judgement.'

Let me give you an example. I was really worried about moving into my new flat. I kept worrying about what the neighbours would be like. Would they be noisy? Would they be homophobic arse wipes who had parties until the early hours? Would they creep into my garden in the early hours and poison all my geraniums?

I moved and they were a bit noisy, they did have some parties. I wasn't any less pissed off about this but the two-week boy Scout in me was prepared for it, so it was much less stressful than it would have been.

Even smaller stresses are easier to manage when you foresee the cyst. Like going out for a date to a restaurant, which you hope will be lovely. You may want charming waiting staff making jokes and flirting with you a little, enough to be flattering but not at all creepy. Food which makes you gasp at the sheer freshness and *joie de vivre*.

Your tongue doing extravagant cha cha cha moves around your mouth it's in so much ecstasy. Humorous and profound conversation with your potential amour and for the restaurant to release a thousand butterflies to dance around as you savour each and every morsel of beauty (the food I mean, not the butterflies).

Sometimes the reality is a crowded, overly illuminated down-at-heel place, where the staff only care about the tips and the food has been defrosted. Your date only eats dates, only talks about the different types of dates they eat but this is not a date-themed restaurant and so therefore no good for eating dates or going on a date.

An utterly crap experience, but if we imagine that it might be stressful then the crapness is not quite so crap.

And yes, I can send a photo of my hands if you'd like.

40. Remove the stressfold

When we're stressed all the good stuff in our life gets put into sharp relief and we forget about anything positive, meaningful or nice.

We don't remember that we're loved by many people, or that we've got a great relationship, or a lovely dog.

The light is obscured by wearing a stressfold. It's like blindfold but more ... well, more stressy.

The stressfold only lets us see darkness. It's right in front of our faces obscuring our view. We have to try and remove the stressfold from our eyes a bit, enough to see the wider picture.

Now, just to be clear this REALLY isn't a case of me saying to you, 'Just look at what lovely summer sandals you've got. Honestly, how can you be stressed when they're so jolly?'

I'm not saying that you just need to be positive. Or to just look on the bright side, because gawd, do I loathe anyone who thinks that's the simple solution to stress. If

I see someone wearing a 'Just be happy' T-shirt, I want to wrangle it from their backs and feed it to a passing moose. I don't do this because that would be wrong, but I really want to.

I was once asked by someone how I was feeling and when I told them my depression was really bad that day, they replied, 'But how can you be depressed on such a sunny day?'

I know. I know.

163

I didn't throw my iced decaf latte at them, which I really should have done, those ice cubes could have done some real damage.

It's also not as simple as practising gratitude (although that will do no harm); it's seeing the broader picture, not the one stress is giving you.

It's **seeing behind the stressfold** – which also happens to be the title of my nine-hundred-page auto-biography, coming out in hardback and available in all good retailers.

To get a better view of our lives we make an honest list of the good stuff. I'll go first shall I, so you can see the kind of thing that I mean and then you can have a go too?

It's fine to include objects, as well as people and places. If your fifty-inch widescreen television with those sur-round sound speakers is important, then put it on the list – the more the merrier.

It should include accomplishments too, that's really crucial. Don't listen to the voice in your head telling you that you've not accomplished anything – you have. If you *really* can't think of anything you've achieved, then you've got through the day so far, and with stress that's a huge accomplishment.

Finally, it's better to do the list when you're not stressed, otherwise the list will be really short, I mean,
you may forget to include your lovely summer sandals. Anyway, here goes.

* My cat
* My husband (probably should have come before the cat)
* My sisters
* My mum
* My nieces and nephew
* My brothers in law
* My friends
* Loving extended family
* My first edition of *I Capture the Castle* by Dodie Smith
* My garden
* A vintage trombone I bought online when I accidently took an extra sleeping pill and was a bit out of it
* My bike